Young Pathfinder 11

A CILT series for primary language teachers

A flying start!

Introducing early language learning

A new edition of *Catching them young* (YPF1)

June de Silva and Peter Satchwell

CiLT The National Centre for Languages

The views expressed in this publication are the authors' and do not necessarily represent those of CILT.

Acknowledgements

The authors wish to thank the CILT editorial team for their constant constructive criticism and many helpful suggestions.

We owe a special debt of gratitude to Dan Tierney (University of Strathclyde) for permission to print in Chapter 5 his invaluable list of child-friendly websites – the result of many hours searching the Internet for sites that are of real use and interest to primary age children.

We also wish to thank Hazel Brent (Head of Languages at Ryton Comprehensive School, Tyne & Wear) for the photographs on p31–32 and her enthusiastic report on the use her school and its feeder primaries are making of the *European Language Portfolio.*

Our thanks are also due to the following primary schools in Surrey and Richmond upon Thames for permission to take and publish some delightful photographs of children in action during foreign language lessons. We have also reproduced children's work from several of these schools:

The Grove Primary School, Camberley; St. Augustine's RC Primary School, Camberley; Ravenscote Primary, Camberley; Lakeside Primary School, Camberley; Trafalgar Junior School, Richmond upon Thames.

The lists of target language in French, German, Spanish (Appendix) are derived from a list published in the *Guide Pédagogique* to *Hélico et ses copains* (Bossus 2001) published by Bordas/ ELI.

First published 1995, second edition 2004, third edition 2008 by CILT, the National Centre for Languages, 111 Westminster Bridge Road, London SE1 7HR

ISBN 13: 978 1 904243 304

A catalogue record for this book is available from the British Library

Series cover design by Neil Alexander
Photography © Barbara Ludman/iwitness 2004

Printed in Great Britain by Hobbs the Printers Ltd.

CILT Publications are available from: Central Books, 99 Wallis Rd, London E9 5LN. Tel: 0845 458 9910. Fax: 0845 458 9912. Book trade representation (UK and Ireland): Broadcast Book Services, Charter House, 29a London Rd, Croydon CR0 2RE. Tel: 020 8681 8949. Fax: 020 8688 0615.

Contents

Introduction

Since we wrote Young Pathfinder 1: *Catching them young* in 1995 much has changed in the field of early language learning (ELL) in the UK and in other European countries. Nine years ago we felt we were really pioneering when CILT publlished the first of the *Young Pathfinder* series, but since the appearance in 2002 of the Government's *National Languages Strategy* we are now on much firmer ground and can look forward, we hope, with some optimism to a properly supported and Government-funded expansion of language learning in our primary schools.

The *National Languages Strategy* makes clear the Government's commitment to primary languages (p15):

> *Delivering an entitlement to language learning so that every pupil at Key Stage 2 is offered the opportunity to study at least one foreign language by the end of the decade is the centrepiece of our strategy. This entitlement is the norm for many of our European partners and most independent schools in our country ...*

> *Every child should have the opportunity throughout KS2 to study a foreign language and develop their interest in the culture of other nations. They should have access to high quality teaching and learning opportunities, making use of native speakers and e-learning. By age 11 they should have the opportunity to reach a recognised level of competence on the Common European Framework and for that achievement to be recognised through a national scheme. The KS2 language learning programme must be delivered, at least in part, in class time.*

This fully revised edition of *Catching them young* sets out to provide help, guidance and encouragement to all primary teachers who are about to embark on a new foreign language programme either at Key Stage 1 (KS1) or Key Stage 2 (KS2). Whether you teach the language on timetable or as a club, we hope you will find help and inspiration here to get you started on planning a coherent language-learning programme for your school(s). For readers who have been teaching a language at primary school for some time, we hope we have provided some new ideas and a pointer to new resources to add to your repertoire.

Our aim in *A flying start!* is to bring you up to date with the current sources of support, continuing professional development opportunities and a range of useful classroom materials; to give you a guide to successful teaching approaches and to provide a practical handbook to help you plan a scheme of work that is appropriate to your particular school.

To put this new edition into context, it is worth taking stock of the progress that has been made since *Catching them young* was first published.

Whereas in 1995 UK primary and secondary schools were still grappling with the ramifications of the National Curriculum and foreign languages were conspicuously absent from the approved primary curriculum, we have experienced since 1997 a considerable shift in attitudes and an ever-increasing interest in ELL, both from parents and from the Government. Now, at last, we have a real commitment to languages for all children at KS2.

In the course of the past 13 years, virtually every European country has made a commitment to teaching languages from age 7 or earlier. In Scotland, a foreign language (French, German, Italian or Spanish) is already on the curriculum of all primary schools; and many of our European neighbours, for example Luxembourg, Italy, Spain, Austria, Croatia, the Netherlands, are light years ahead of us in this field.

If we are to raise the profile of early language learning in this country to reach the target set out in the *National Languages Strategy* – entitlement to languages for all from age 7 by 2010, we have to spread the good practice that already exists, with some 70% of English primary schools now providing languages teaching in class time.

A great deal of valuable development work has been done in the past few years to establish what methods and approaches work in primary classrooms – and resources for ELL have improved enormously. Thanks to CILT, the Qualifications and Curriculum Authority (QCA) and a variety of publishers great and small, a wealth of good quality teaching material and sound advice on methodology is now available to primary teachers.

The publication in 2005/2006 by the DfES of The Keystage 2 Framework for Languages is a key development. The Framework provides significant encouragement and clear guidance to all primary schools in England in planning the introduction of languages into their curriculum by 2010.

The Framework is published in three parts:

Part 1 sets out detailed Learning Objectives for Years 3, 4, 5 and 6. Each year's work is defined under five aspects or strands: Oracy, Literacy, Intercultural Understanding, Knowledge about Language (KAL) and Language Learning Strategies (LLS).

Part 2 contains an introduction to the Framework for all users; helpful advice to Headteachers, Senior Managers and Subject-Coordinators; advice to schools and teachers introducing languages for the first time; advice to those schools who are already teaching languages, and advice for secondary schools on supporting Primary Entitlement.

Part 3 offers guidance on using the Framework as a planning tool; whole school planning, integrating languages with the rest of the curriculum; advice on inclusion – meeting the needs of all children, including those for whom English is an additional language; progression; transition and continuity; assessment and recording, and working together – using the Framework in different contexts, including mixed age classes and small schools.

The Framework is available in hard copy and online as part of the Primary materials on the Standards site **www.standards.dfes.gov.uk/primary/languages**

The website **www.primarylanguages.org.uk** which has been developed by CILT for primary leaders, teachers and trainers forms a major element in the national programme of training for primary teachers and will provide access to ongoing help on ELL methodology and CPD.

The KS2 Framework for Languages is intended to provide teachers with a resource from which to create their own schemes of work. It is meant to be a climbing frame, not a strait-jacket. It is not prescriptive; on the contrary, it is intended "to give teachers the freedom to be creative and innovative." So schools should "feel free to create their own courses and teaching/learning activities suited to the experiences and interests of their own children."

We would therefore recommend all primary schools to study the Framework carefully before setting out their plans for languages by September 2009. This applies equally to those schools just starting (at KS1 or at KS2) as well as to those who have been teaching languages at KS2 for some time

As in the first edition of this book, we have focused on the importance of careful preparation before embarking on a new language programme, essential planning for progression, successful methodology and the use of the target language in class. We have added a substantial chapter on finding support and resources, as we feel it is essential for every primary teacher to feel confident and secure in what he or she is doing in the languages classroom.

In writing this book we have tried to combine our own two perspectives on early language learning – one of the adviser observing and evaluating a variety of primary teachers at work in the classroom and the other of the ELL practitioner looking out from her own French classes in a cluster of primary schools. We hope that the result will provoke reflection and a spark of enthusiasm in our readers.

As a measure of the change that has taken place in ELL in recent years we have presented overleaf the key developments that have increased both our knowledge and experience of good practice in teaching languages in primary schools – developments that have persuaded the Government to back the expansion of language learning to all primary schools and encouraged several Local Education Authorities (LEAs) to put money and support staff into exciting local initiatives which are already producing real results and rewarding learning experiences for young pupils and teachers alike.

Milestones in the development of early

1997

CILT organises the first **Primary Languages Show** in Southampton. This is now an annual two-day event, held in March in Manchester.

1998

The **Nuffield Languages Inquiry** is set up to report to the Government on the language capability and language needs of the UK.

The **DfEE** funds research into good practice in ELL.

1999

A new **National Advisory Centre on Early Language Learning (NACELL)** is established within CILT.

CILT sets up the **NACELL information unit** in the CILT Resources Library, the **NACELL website** and the **ELL e-mail discussion forum**. The *Early Language Learning Bulletin* is published three times a year.

CILT sets up and manages the **Good Practice Project (GPP)** over two years. Eighteen schools/LEAs report monthly on progress in their schools covering: staffing arrangements, resources for teacher training, classroom resources and teaching approaches, continuity and transfer to secondary schools.

The **Qualifications and Curriculum Authority (QCA)** publishes **curriculum guidance** and a **Scheme of Work for languages at KS2**.

1999 onwards

In collaboration with the French, Spanish and German cultural institutes, **CILT** sets up **annual residential INSET courses abroad for primary teachers**.

2000

Publication of the **Nuffield Languages Inquiry** final report, *Languages: the next generation*. Among many far-reaching recommendations it urges the Government to make a long-term commitment to ELL and declare a ten-year target to provide entitlement for all primary pupils from age 7.

The DfEE begins the appointment of **Advanced Skills Teachers**, including some to teach foreign languages in primary schools.

CILT Comenius Centres in England and Wales **offer training and support** for primary languages teachers.

2000–2002

CILT manages the piloting of the *European Languages Portfolio* in several UK primary schools.

2001

The **Good Practice Project** proves so successful that the DfES provides further funding to extend the research project to other schools and LEAs.

The **Teacher Training Agency (TTA) and CILT** work with five higher education colleges to develop a **French specialist module within primary PGCE courses**.

The *European Languages Portfolio – Junior version* is published by CILT and is made available on the NACELL website.

2001–2003

The Development of Early Language Learning (DELL) Project builds on the evidence and experience of the Good Practice Project.

CILT produces the first of three **ELL INSET videos** to provide teachers with examples of good practice and patterns of provision from Nursery classes to KS2, showing teachers from the GPP and DELL projects in action.

2002

CILT publishes a set of *Curricular models* on the NACELL website based on the successful experience of the GPP/DELL projects.

language learning: 1997–2004

The Government publishes *Languages for all: Languages for life – A strategy for England* setting out its commitment to improve language-learning provision, especially in primary schools and declares a commitment to provide **entitlement to language learning for all primary pupils at KS2 from 2010**.

2003

157 Specialist Language Colleges in England are given a special responsibility for co-ordination and co-operation with their feeder primary schools in order to create coherent foreign languages programmes across the divide: the ELL-Languages College project.

Expansion of the **initial teacher training** programme to **nearly 500 places on Primary PGCE courses at 26 Higher Education Institutions.** Reciprocal teacher training programmes now expanded to include Germany and Spain.

Government appoints a **National Director for Languages** (Dr Lid King) to head **the National Languages Strategy**.

Government makes commitment to creating a new **National Ladder of Achievement**: a recognition system for language learners from primary to adult level. Pilot 2003/2004, national launch: 2005.

CILT publishes the *NACELL best practice guide* for primary teachers on the NACELL website.

DfES funds **19 LEA Primary Pathfinder schemes** to expand and disseminate good practice to more areas of the country.

119 Advanced Skills Teachers (ASTs) for primary languages appointed.

The new national '**Languages Ladder – steps to success' is trialled** in 20 schools.

2005

ITT primary project expands to include Italy and Portugal, as well as France, Germany and Spain.

Languages Ladder launched May 2005.

KS2 Framework for Languages and DfES Evaluation of the KS2 Language Learning Pathfinders published.

Over 260 primary schools employ FLAs.

2006–2007

DfES/TDA Primary CPD and DFES HLTA/TA course materials produced. **www.nacell.org.uk/profdev/profdev.htm**

Junior European Language Portfolio is revised in the light of the Framework and Languages Ladder.

DfES Audit of language learning provision at Key Stage 2 **www.dfes.gov.uk/research/programmeofresearch/index.cfm?type=0**

DfES Longitudinal investigation of language learning at Key Stage 2 **www.dfes.gov.uk/research/programmeofresearch/index.cfm?type=0**

CILT launches the Primary Languages website.

QCA produces revised schemes of work for French (available 2006), German and Spanish (available 2007).

1. Making a start

 ## WHY START EARLY?

EVERYONE ELSE IS DOING IT

In the past fifteen years there has been increasing evidence from researchers and classroom teachers in the UK and many other countries (Australia, Canada, Scotland and many of our European neighbours) that there are distinct advantages in 'catching them young'.

The expansion of early language learning across most of Europe has been quite dramatic and parents in areas of the UK where primary schools have woven a foreign language into the curriculum have been very supportive.

YOUNG CHILDREN ARE NATURALLY ADEPT AT IT

We all know that young children start to develop their mother-tongue language skills from the age of one; that by the age of 18 months many children have already acquired a vocabulary of over 100 words and by the age of 2 some bright children have progressed to an amazing range of coherent sentences and questions, even devising their own versions of past and future tenses. Their capacity for accurate mimicry of phrases that they have never heard before is sometimes astounding.

Teachers and parents who expose their children to a second language early in childhood soon realise that this innate gift of mimicry enables 2, 3 and 4 year-olds to pick up songs and rhymes in a foreign language without any difficulty, provided that they are repeated often enough and are associated with actions and a sense of fun. (There are lovely examples of a Reception class singing a Spanish song with gusto and playing a playground clapping game on the CILT Early Language Learning videos 2 and 3 – Making it work and Making it better.)

LANGUAGE LEARNING SHOULD BE PART OF EVERY CHILD'S DEVELOPMENT

The case for an early start with languages has been made by many organisations in the past few years, including the National Association of Headteachers, CILT, the Association for Language Learning, QCA – and even the Prime Minister.

The Primary Languages Network, set up in the 1980s as a 'think tank' on early language learning issues, has acted for fifteen years as a voluntary working party of teacher trainers, advisers, Advisory Teachers, researchers and primary project co-ordinators. In 1997, it lobbied David Blunkett and the DfEE for a more positive approach to language learning in primary schools. The following rationale was set out in a consultation paper sent to the DfEE in 1997:

The introduction of foreign languages into the primary school curriculum

Foreign language learning provides a valuable educational, social and cultural experience for all children, developing life skills, general learning skills and awareness of how language works. The learning of a new language makes a major contribution to the development of the whole child.

Linguistic development

The development of oracy and literacy is a priority for all children. As many start school with very poor communication skills, learning a foreign language can make a major contribution to their general language development – in both mother tongue and the foreign language.

Learning a new language can help reinforce skills and concepts introduced in the mother tongue in other curriculum areas.

Learning one foreign language at primary school lays the foundations for the acquisition of other languages later in life.

Cultural development

Children entering primary school in the 21st century will be expected to live and ultimately work in a multicultural, multilingual European community. An international dimension should be an integral part of the primary curriculum in order to raise children's awareness of how other people in the world live and think. Learning another language develops children's understanding of the wider world by offering insights into their own and foreign cultures.

Personal and social development

Interaction between teacher and pupils forms a major part of language learning, involving constant rehearsal and performance, which can enhance self-esteem.

Children gain the confidence to speak in front of others, to perform in pairs or small groups, in class and in public.

We shall return to these aspects of pupil development in our discussion of aims and objectives of early language learning later in this chapter.

AN EARLY START CREATES POSITIVE ATTITUDES AND MOTIVATION

In 1998, after ten years of the development phase of the Scottish Modern Languages in the Primary School project (piloted 1989–1994, extended to all primary schools from 1995), Her Majesty's Inspectors were able to report on the 'enthusiasm and motivation of almost all pupils in the primary schools, high attainment by some very able pupils, examples of good or very good language teaching in 85% of schools, and very good organisation of resources and classroom display'.

WHERE DO WE BEGIN?

Before embarking on a foreign languages project, your school will have to tackle some key organisational questions and make decisions on a number of important issues. These are decisions that you cannot make on your own. Weaving a new language into the curriculum will have an impact on the work of all your colleagues. So the senior management and, ideally, the rest of the staff need to be involved in discussing how the language will be fitted into the 'already overcrowded' school week.

THINGS TO THINK ABOUT BEFORE YOU BEGIN

WHEN CAN WE START?

You will need several months of **planning time** to:

- gather ideas on methods;
- collect resources;
- find what INSET courses are accessible to you;
- obtain practical help from other language teachers;
- discuss your plans with colleagues;
- create a scheme of work.

WHICH LANGUAGE CAN WE OFFER?

This will be decided first and foremost by the level of languages expertise/confidence of your current staff and their willingness to start teaching a language. The introduction of a new language is, of course, not something to be taken on lightly! This may well also restrict the number of classes to be taught in the first year of the project. We suggest starting small – with your youngest year-group only – and slowly working your way up, as and when you are all more confident.

You will also need to consult your local secondary schools from the outset to share with them your plans and ensure that they are supportive of your choice of language and your outline scheme of work.

If you are fortunate to be a feeder primary school to a Specialist Languages College you should be able to enlist real practical help in the form of some teaching and consultation time from one of their language specialists.

Whatever your circumstances, make sure you find a native speaker, a Foreign Language Assistant or a secondary colleague to act as your 'linguistic consultant!' (see Chapter 4).

WHO WILL BE ABLE TO TEACH THE FOREIGN LANGUAGE? AT WHAT LEVEL?

This will of course depend on the initial training and/or previous experience of your colleagues. If no one but you has had any foreign language training, you are on your own! However, many primary teachers who were keen to set up a project in their school in spite of no formal teaching qualifications in a language, have made the effort to find in-service training (e.g. at a local LEA or CILT Early Language Learning Regional Support Group, or on a CILT course abroad) and come back enthusiastic to set up the language in their own classroom (see also Chapter 4).

It might be wise to do an audit to establish what linguistic talents are lying hidden in the school and what the refreshment needs of each individual teacher would be. In some schools it may be wise to start with relatively simple activities at Key Stage 1 and gradually progress to Key Stage 2 as staff confidence and expertise increase.

WHAT SORT OF TRAINING WILL THOSE TEACHERS NEED?

First and foremost, teachers will need linguistic refreshment in the areas of competence outlined in Chapter 4, 'What do I need to know?'.

Secondly, teachers will need some cultural updating in the topic areas listed on p14, especially if they have not visited the foreign country concerned in recent years.

Thirdly, and most importantly, teachers will need methodological guidance and advice on what is now established good practice in language teaching for the target age group.

While much can be gained from consulting books (e.g. CILT *Young Pathfinders*, *Modern Foreign Languages in the primary school* (Sharpe 2001)) and the NACELL website, there is no substitute for good hands-on INSET of the kind organised at CILT ELL Regional Support Groups or on CILT/Embassy summer courses abroad.

Long before there was any national backing for primary languages, several LEAs, such as Kent, Surrey, West Sussex, South Gloucestershire and Richmond upon Thames, had set up primary languages projects on their own initiative and appointed Advisory Teachers to co-ordinate in-service training and support individual teachers in the classroom.

Over the past ten years Kent LEA, for example, has provided a modest INSET package for non-specialist primary teachers that has enabled over 400 primary schools to embark on French, German or Spanish, based round the video teaching materials in *Pilote, 3, 2, 1 los!* and *Tú y yo*.

Liverpool LEA is now providing similar INSET through its Advisory Teachers who team-teach in the classroom with Foreign Language Assistants and the classteacher, as well as providing linguistic and methodological training sessions.

WHERE AND WHEN WILL INSET BE AVAILABLE?

It is important for teachers to find training and/or linguistic refreshment in advance of the launch date of the planned project. You will need to find out whether your LEA already runs courses for primary languages. If not, contact your nearest Comenius Centre or CILT ELL Regional Support Group, which offer free twilight INSET sessions. The number of Regional Support Groups has increased to 75, covering most areas of England.

You will need your headteacher's blessing and funding to attend INSET, so any project you start needs to be part of the School Development Plan. If you can, try to get on one of the CILT summer courses in France, Germany, Italy or Spain.

Do not hesitate to contact other schools in your area who have already started teaching a language. They are bound to be a source of useful advice.

HOW LONG WILL THE FOREIGN LANGUAGE EXPERIENCE BE – ONE YEAR OR MORE?

Planning and resourcing one year's work will be a big enough task, but your school will need to think about the 'domino effect' of successive year groups continuing the language after the initial set-up year, whether they started in Reception, KS1 or KS2.

In any case you will need a detailed plan for the first year and an outline plan for the same classes continuing into their second year. This has resource implications (see Chapter 2, 'Planning for progression')!

HOW WILL THE PROJECT BE RESOURCED?

A worthwhile language project cannot be run on a shoestring! You will need to negotiate with your headteacher a realistic allocation of funds to create an adequate stock of teaching materials in order to start – and you will need top-up funds to add to your repertoire over two or three years thereafter. The *National Languages Strategy* makes it clear that responsibility for setting up primary languages in the next six years will rest with LEAs and headteachers, so that is where you start!

CURRICULUM TIME

Most schools find a way of creating space for foreign language learning, even if it is only a few minutes a day. There are many models of provision across the country and schools eventually work out a system that suits them. In Scotland a foreign language is already part of the curriculum for all pupils in Years 6 and 7 (transfer to secondary is at age 12). Many Scottish schools, for example, allocate 80–90 minutes a week (two 45-minute lessons) as discrete foreign language slots; other schools prefer 10–15 minutes a day fitted in as refreshers at the start of the day or between other curriculum activities.

You can see some of the possible variations on the NACELL website: *Curricular models* (**www. nacell.org.uk/bestpractice/models.htm**). You will find here examples of individual primary schools, partnership models where a secondary school works with a cluster of primaries and LEA models. All are described in some detail, including the financial aspects.

If you teach off timetable as a club, we would recommend two short sessions a week rather than one longer one.

In view of the considerable common ground between teaching English and a foreign language you should certainly find plenty of scope to make foreign language work part and parcel of your Literacy Hour, raising children's awareness of language on the broadest front (see Young Pathfinder 9: *The literacy link*).

DESIGNING YOUR OWN SCHEME OF WORK

It goes without saying that the circumstances and requirements of one primary school can differ considerably from the next one down the road. It is not possible therefore to present here an 'off-the-shelf' model of a scheme of work that you can use next year. You will have to think out and write up your own tailor-made version, reflecting the needs of your school and the children you are planning to teach.

However, we would point all teachers to the very helpful 'Scheme of Work for languages at KS2' published by QCA in 2000. This document is a really excellent starting point for producing your own scheme and provides a model layout for a detailed programme of work over one, two or three years. It provides twelve units, worked out fully for French, German and Spanish.

You will find really helpful examples of KS1 schemes of work in the *NACELL best practice guide* (**www.nacell.org.uk**).

You will also need to think about your aims and objectives in introducing children to a foreign language. We have set out some ideas below to provide you with a starting point and to stimulate discussion with your colleagues. These ideas have acquired fairly universal international currency in the last few years and many of them are contained in the *Nürnberg recommendations on early language learning (Die Nürnberger Empfehlungen zum frühen Fremdsprachenlernen)* put together by a European Working group of primary experts and published by the Goethe-Institut in 1996 (**www.goethe.de/z/50/pub/nuernb**).

These recommendations were developed in a series of international symposiums of 25 experts in the teaching of German as a foreign language from 18 European countries and the USA. They set out a clear rationale for ELL, clear aims and the basic principles of ELL methodology. They are used in many European primary schools and form the basis of much ELL teaching on the European continent.

KEY AIMS OF EARLY LANGUAGE LEARNING

Awakening children's interest in another language

Encouraging communicative behaviour

Learning how to learn

The learning of the language itself

Fostering intercultural ways of looking at things

GENERAL AIMS OF AN EARLY LANGUAGE-LEARNING PROGRAMME

Children's first encounter with a foreign language should:

- make an important contribution to the development of the whole child and thereby promote his or her emotional, creative, social, cognitive and linguistic capabilities;
- give children the basic foundations of the foreign language and show ways in which it is used to communicate in everyday life;
- awaken interest in languages and develop enjoyment in learning them;
- enable children to experience and use the language as a means of communication, learning to operate within the framework of certain conventions (e.g. tu/vous) so that they succeed in making themselves understood. This requires a modicum of accuracy!;
- motivate children to express themselves in a language other than their own;
- make them more aware of how their own language works;
- give children an additional opportunity to see the world from a different point of view, to open their minds to different cultures and to find their way in the world;
- enable children to experience another culture and its related social customs, thereby raising their awareness of their own culture – and adding an intercultural, international dimension to the curriculum;
- give the children the experience of learning strategies that help to increase their ability to work independently.

You will no doubt wish to present some of these ideas more simply in your own document – and omit some if they do not seem appropriate.

The same will apply to the objectives we have listed below. These are just a few of the possibilities that we have gleaned from primary teachers over a number of years.

OBJECTIVES

Our ELL scheme sets out to:

- develop confidence in listening skills and the ability to listen attentively;
- involve children in active learning, using a multi-sensory approach;
- develop a sense of fun and enthusiasm for language learning;
- develop real accuracy in speaking skills, providing intensive practice and repetition to hone pronunciation, intonation, rhythm and stress patterns;
- help children to match sounds to the printed word;
- develop self-confidence in speaking the foreign language;

- develop a real sense of achievement;
- develop the ability to find out new words and facts for themselves;
- provide constant revision and reinforcement opportunities for all abilities;
- create a warm, supportive and rewarding atmosphere in the classroom;
- create a classroom and school environment where the use of the foreign language in everyday communication is obviously valued.

Teachers will find further advice in the forthcoming KS2 Framework (currently being developed and due to be launched in 2005). This will deal with the issues of oracy, literacy, language awareness and cultural awareness.

 ## TEACHING APPROACHES AND PRIMARY METHODOLOGY

Your approach to teaching the language will obviously be dictated by the age, stage of development and the interests and ability of your particular class, but the aims and objectives we have suggested above bring with them significant methodological implications. As Keith Sharpe (2001) has pointed out on many occasions: 'Primary French tends (and needs) to be more primary than French'; in other words, the whole approach to languages in the primary school needs to be founded on good primary practice – the principle that the class teacher knows his or her pupils well, knows what motivates them and is able to use methods from all curriculum areas which will sustain their interest and ensure progress.

If we are to educate the whole child and build up his or her confidence, developing cognitive and general learning skills, we need to think about:

- **classroom atmosphere:** creating an environment in which each individual can experience success and develop self-confidence;
- **multi-sensory learning:** providing a stimulating programme of child-centred activities that promote enjoyment as well as providing a challenge (listening, speaking, reciting, story-telling, singing, miming, acting, playing games, making things);
- **embedding:** integrating the foreign language into aspects of daily class routines and, wherever possible, into other areas of the primary curriculum (register, collecting dinner money, class organisation, date, weather chart, drama, music, science, artwork, ICT, PE, games played inside and out);
- **experiencing success:** ensuring a sense of achievement for all (setting performance tasks that are achievable, rewarding children for what they can do in the foreign language, providing differentiated tasks that lead to some learner independence: pairwork, groupwork);
- **progress:** building in real progression and continuity over time (a planned scheme of work, systematic build-up of structures and vocabulary that enables the learners to say what **they** want to say in the foreign language).

CHOOSING YOUR TOPICS/THEMES

The diagram below illustrates the topics that seem to form the kernel of most European primary languages schemes. The list is by no means exhaustive and you will no doubt think of other possibilities that will interest your classes. In fact many other variations on these themes can be found in primary teaching materials produced in France, Germany, Italy and Spain (see Chapter 5).

THEMES AND TOPICS

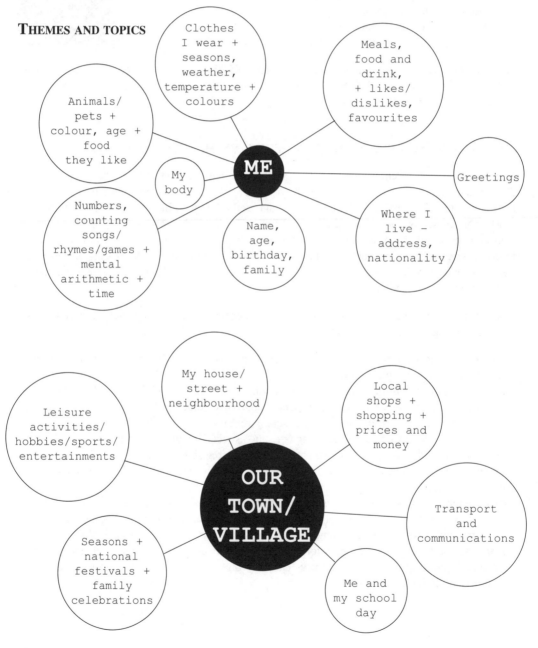

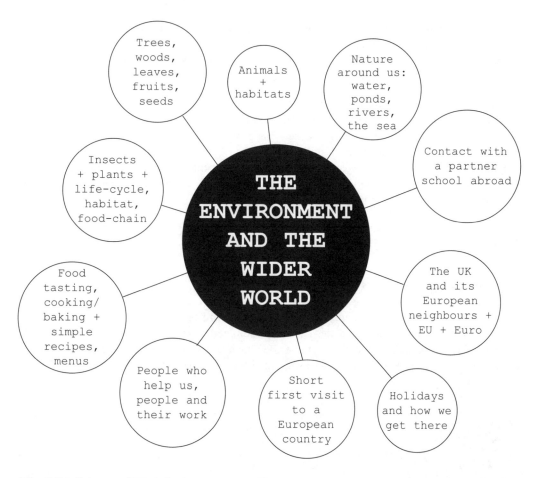

The QCA Scheme of Work for languages at KS2 sets out twelve notional units of work covering most of the areas in our diagram. However, there is at least two to three years' work in these twelve units, as QCA points out in the *Teacher's guide*, and we would not recommend attempting more than four or five broad topic areas in one school year.

If you are starting with a Nursery, Reception or KS1 class, we would recommend a rather different approach. You may well find it more appropriate to link the topics you choose directly to the themes the children have just covered in other curriculum areas, e.g. number work, shapes, stories and characters they already know.

Young Pathfinder 9: *The literacy link* (Cheater and Farren 2001) suggests many ideas for work at word, sentence and text level.

'The language-learning-process should challenge and extend them, appeal to their feelings, develop their motivation, their imagination and their creativity. And of course their enjoyment' (Goethe-Institut 1996). We would add that, wherever possible, the foreign language programme should overlap with and reinforce concepts and ideas that the children have already encountered, or are currently learning, in their mother tongue. As Richard Johnstone (1994b) points out, 'the purpose of learning a foreign language is not just to learn the language but also to experience or learn something about life through the language.'

The *Nürnberg recommendations* further suggest that the content of ELL should come from children's literature, science and geography/environmental studies, depending on the interests of a particular class. If you are the class teacher, this gives you scope for positive cross-curricular work, building on the concepts and skills the children have already acquired in their mother tongue. If you are a peripatetic 'Spanish-and-vanish' teacher, this implies close collaboration with the class teacher to ensure you know what topics have already been covered, and in what ways you can reinforce and extend the children's knowledge through work in the foreign language'.

You will find a wealth of possibilities for cross-curricular work set out in Young Pathfinder 7: *Making the link* (Tierney and Hope 1998).

 ## PLANNING THE TIMESCALE

Having identified your broad themes for the year, you will need to find appropriate classroom resources and plan a notional timescale. There is a useful template for a planning grid in the QCA Scheme of Work for KS2. You will need to decide which is the most useful format that will work for you and your colleagues, but we have suggested two possible versions opposite.

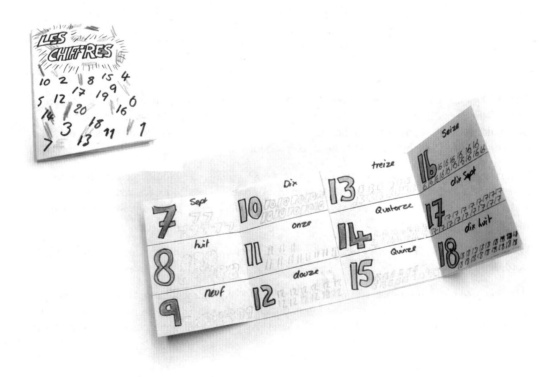

SAMPLE PLANNING GRIDS

A

Week	Lesson	New language	Key structures	Pupil activities	Resources
9	1	family members	*voici ma mère, voici mon père*	pupils draw portraits or bring photos of own family	flashcards/photos/cartoons
		numbers 22–31	*les numéros 22–31 nous allons compter de 20–30, de 31–20*		number fans
		colours	*les couleurs de l'arc-en ciel: rouge, jaune, etc*	pupils make rainbow collage	colour cards and felt-tips
		preferences	*j'aime, je n'aime pas je préfère ... le violet*	Class survey: *notre couleur préférée*	paints
		months	*les mois de l'année un calendrier*	pupils make months mobile, word seasons collage	word cards

LEARNING OBJECTIVES/TEACHING OBJECTIVES/LEARNING OUTCOMES

B

LEARNING OBJECTIVES	TEACHING OBJECTIVES	LEARNING OUTCOMES
Children should learn to:	**Method:**	**Children can:**
Introduce family members	Take fictitious family (e.g. Simpsons) to practise *Qui est-ce? C'est le père,* etc	Identify correct names of family members
Say today's date	Practise: *On est quel jour aujourd'hui? C'est le lundi 14 juillet*	Identify the days of the week, recite them in order, sing them – ditto with months. Say date of own birthday

2. Progression

 HOW DO WE DEFINE PROGRESSION IN EARLY LANGUAGE LEARNING?

Wherever your pupils begin their first encounter with a foreign language, whether it be at Nursery, in the Reception class or in Key Stage 2, they will need to progress on several fronts: linguistically, emotionally, and in terms of learning skills and developing self-confidence.

Linguistically the children need to progress from initial recognition and understanding of single words to short phrases, questions and answers, through to understanding whole sentences – and eventually, before the end of KS2, to tackling short texts of, say, five or six sentences (e.g. understanding a postcard or simple letter, a description of a person or a place).

They also need to progress from very simple, child-centred text (e.g. cartoon speech bubbles, simple rhymes and songs) to more sophisticated descriptive language in texts that inform them about real life in the wider world outside (e.g. foreign children's diaries of their school day, their hobbies, or a description of their town/village).

The nature and the challenge of the tasks that the children are set also needs to progress from the very simplest: *listen and repeat; listen and colour in; listen and do the action (clap, stamp, jump ...),* to more challenging ones which require more than one skill: *listen to the story, read the sentences and then put them in order; listen to the tape, read the sentences and complete the descriptions of these children ...*

There needs to be progression also in the content of the texts that children encounter, starting at Key Stage 1 with very simple rhymes and songs and games, visuals and cartoons that reflect the children's interests and experiences of the world, but gradually introducing concepts and ideas which they may have encountered in other curriculum areas.

Traditionally, language teachers have concentrated on the four specific language skills of Listening, Speaking, Reading and Writing, but there is more to language learning than that and, if they are to become successful and enthusiastic learners, young children will need to acquire other skills – skills that are also a crucial part of child development in primary school.

They will need **general learning skills** – learning:

- to concentrate;
- to listen attentively;
- to respond appropriately to a variety of aural stimuli (listen and do: 'Simon says');
- and eventually learning to work independently of the teacher to look up and find out things for themselves (using a picture dictionary, using the Internet).

As an essential part of their own development children also need to acquire **social skills** – learning how:

- to listen to others;
- to take turns;
- to speak up and speak clearly;
- to work in pairs or groups and to help each other.

The foreign language lesson is also an opportunity to boost children's **self-confidence** – encouraging them to get their tongue round new sounds, to have a go in the new language, to speak to a puppet or to a native speaker, to recite a rhyme or sing a song, to **perform** in class – and eventually in public. And they will eventually want to express their feelings and emotions in the new language, their likes, dislikes, sadness sometimes, and their enjoyment.

We should make sure too that our language lessons build in opportunities for the children to confront foreignness ('otherness') in a non-threatening way. It is in the primary school that we have a golden opportunity to start children thinking about other traditions and cultures in the world and to raise their awareness that not every country shares the way of life of the UK. By encouraging your pupils to talk about and share their encounters with traditions and languages from other parts of the world, you will find that young children are often capable of showing real empathy with people from other countries and surprising insights into the nature of language learning.

There is a fascinating discussion in Young Pathfinder 10: *A world of languages* (Datta and Pomphrey 2004) of children's awareness of language diversity – with examples of children's perceptions of what it is like to start to learn a new language in a multicultural society.

 ## PLANNING FOR PROGRESSION

In this chapter we will attempt to define some of the differences between teaching very young children – in Nursery, Reception and KS1 classes – and teaching 7–10 year-olds at KS2. We hope this will encourage teachers to think carefully about their own planning, to make sure that their expectations are realistic for the age group they are teaching, but at the same time stimulating and challenging to the children.

KS1 APPRENTICESHIP

For many years Eric Hawkins, our leading authority on language learning in the UK (Emeritus Professor and former Director of the Language Centre at the University of York) has talked about *apprentissage*; the idea that the children's first encounter with a new language should be an apprenticeship in learning how to learn a language (Hawkins 1987). And that very first step involves a 're-education of the ear'. Many children, sadly, start school with very poor oral and aural skills in their mother tongue. So anything that we do in the foreign language lesson should, ideally, try to complement and enhance those skills.

Our apprenticeship should therefore include:

- learning to sit still and listen attentively;
- hearing new sounds accurately;
- mimicking new sounds – with lots of repetition!;
- getting our tongue round new sounds, new consonant clusters (*zu, zwei, zwischen, zwitschern, Stein, ich ...; paella, niño, Xavier, Juan-Carlos, mujer ...*) or totally new vowel sounds (*un, une, on, an, vin, nounours, écureuil ... ; cuando, tiene, indio ...*);
- picking up new intonation patterns – hearing the stress on the last syllable of most French words (*ani<u>mal</u>, nou<u>nours</u>, croco<u>dile</u>, élé<u>phant</u> ...*) and, of course, the rise in intonation to make questions (*Ça <u>va</u>? Tu as <u>fi</u>ni? Quel est ton numé<u>ro</u>?*);
- listening for and recognising words that rhyme (*un éléphant qui est méchant ...; die Katzen haben schwarze Tatzen ...; en abril, aguas mil ...*);
- memorising simple foreign language rhymes, *comptines*, songs – and performing them as a class or in groups, e.g.

Qui vient tous les matins,	*Pito, pito, gogorito.*
Dans mon jardin,	*¿Dónde vas tú tan bonito?*
Manger des carottes et du pain?	*En la era verdadera.*
C'est le lapin.	*Pin, pon, fuera.*

- learning activity songs and rhymes so that the language is associated with physical actions ('Head, shoulders, knees and toes'; *'Frère Jacques'; 'Eins, zwei, Polizei'; 'Cabeza, cintura, rodillas y pies' ...*);
- counting in groups: 0–5, 5–10, 10–20, forwards and backwards, and then using the numbers to do simple mental arithmetic (*2 et 3 font 5; 6 minus 4 macht 2; 5 y 3 son 8*);
- listen and repeat, then listen and respond with your own answer.

Most of what we do in the foreign language at KS1 should be based firmly on the skills development that underlies the rest of the primary curriculum. Wherever we can reinforce skills and concepts already learnt in Maths, English, Science, etc we should seize the opportunity to use the existing equipment and adapt the materials already in school to follow up in the foreign language lessons. So, for example, all the work that children do on numbers, shapes, colours can be repeated and consolidated in language lessons. Simple science experiments such as sinking and floating, or sowing seeds and measuring growth rates of seedlings, can easily be carried out in a foreign language. (For a very detailed discussion of links with literacy and numeracy in foreign languages see Young Pathfinder 9: *The literacy link* (Cheater and Farren 2001)).

We would suggest that work in KS1 should concentrate on developing skills – and that the content you choose should relate closely to the children's world, e.g.

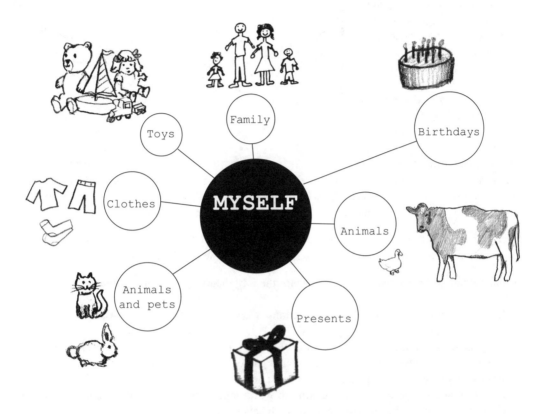

Children need to be active and involved, singing, playing games, performing whenever possible. Many multi-sensory activities from the Nursery and Reception can be recycled in the foreign language:

- 'What's in the bag?';
- skipping games, 'Hopscotch';
- 'When you hear an odd number/an even number/your colour, jump or wave!'.

You will find really helpful examples of KS1 schemes of work on the NACELL website in the *NACELL best practice guide* (which can be downloaded free of charge from **www.nacell.org. uk**).

Many imaginative and well-tried activities for the youngest children in Nursery and KS1 classes are available in the materials produced by La Jolie Ronde (e.g. *Entre dans la ronde* and *La ronde des petits*) and Merryman Primary Resources (e.g. *Chante Noël!* and *Ouvre la porte!*).

LISTENING, SPEAKING, READING AND WRITING – THE FOUR LANGUAGE-LEARNING SKILLS

In the course of the children's first year of language learning we should of course concentrate above all on Listening and Speaking. But that does not mean that the children should never see the printed word or be discouraged from reading aloud labels, captions and short sentences. On the contrary, many children find that relating

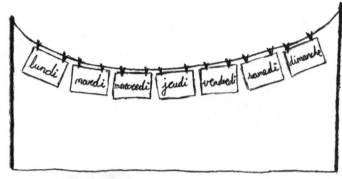

the sound to the printed word provides a useful *aide-mémoire*. So hanging balloons and mobiles with the colours or your classroom calendar with the days of the week/simple weather phrases printed on them, or your washing line with the new words pegged up will all contribute to memorisation.

Depending on each school's circumstances and, of course, the time allocated to language lessons we would hope that by the end of their first year most of the children could:

- understand simple songs and rhymes, learn them by heart and perform them – as a group or solo;
- listen and do: i.e. carry out simple instructions: *Viens ici! Touche le genou! Assieds-toi!* … and play simple games such as 'Simon says';
- carry out class routines: e.g. *Lève le doigt! Ferme la porte! Donne-moi un crayon bleu!;*
- listen and play: classroom games, playground games;
- listen and sing along with teacher and/or cassette;
- recognise and use foreign words relating to work done in other areas of the curriculum: e.g. colours of rainbow, shapes, numbers/sums, alphabet …;
- recognise key words when seen in print/on display as captions, labels, mobiles or friezes (days, months, weather, clothes …).

For example:

IN FRENCH/GERMAN/ ITALIAN/SPANISH

I can …

- ☐ Say hello!
- ☐ Say my name.
- ☐ Ask someone how he or she is.
- ☐ Say I am well.
- ☐ Say goodbye.
- ☐ Say six colours.

- ☐ These are the colours I know …
- ☐ Count from 0 to 6.
- ☐ Count from 7 to 12.
- ☐ Say how old I am.
- ☐ Ask someone how old he or she is.

- ☐ Say which month my birthday is in.
- ☐ Say all the months.
- ☐ Say what day it is today.
- ☐ Say all the days of the week.

This is only one of many possible ways of recording pupils' progress. The European Language Portfolio contains several ready-made profile sheets for children to complete as part of their Language Biography and pages like the one we have reproduced here (filled in by Jessica, aged 9) can easily be adapted to suit your particular class at the end of a term or year (see also p30).

KS2 CHILDREN DEVELOPING AS LANGUAGE LEARNERS

In the Teacher's Guide to the QCA Scheme of Work for KS2 there is a very helpful table in *Appendix 1: Progression in early language learning.* This sets out clearly ways in which children may progress as beginners in language learning. In our abbreviated version of this table overleaf, we have identified where these skills might be most appropriately introduced over both Key Stages.

PROGRESSION IN LANGUAGE SKILLS AND LANGUAGE-LEARNING SKILLS

Teaching children how to listen carefully	KS1
Promoting experimentation with the new sound system	KS1
Encouraging accurate pronunciation/intonation	KS1
Using a variety of authentic listening texts to train the ear	KS1 + 2
Training children to memorise efficiently	KS1 + 2
Showing children how new language can be integrated into previously learnt language in a growing range of differentcontexts	KS2
Increasing the length of sentences and texts that children hear	KS2
Increasing the range of contexts and speakers – and the range of tasks	KS2
Linking the sound with the spelling of the new vocabulary	KS1 + 2
Teaching children how to use dictionaries and other reference materials	KS2
Consolidating new vocabulary and structures regularly	KS1 + 2
Teaching children how to learn and record new items of language	KS1 + 2
Promoting creative use of the new language	KS1 + 2

PROGRESSION IN UNDERSTANDING, LEARNING AND APPLYING SIMPLE ASPECTS OF GRAMMAR

Introducing a grammatical point in a relevant and meaningful context	KS1 + 2
Encouraging comparison with English or another language	KS1 + 2
Encouraging discussion about how words and sentences are constructed	KS1 + 2
Drawing conclusions, understanding, learning and applying simple grammatical rules	KS2
Providing opportunities for manipulating language and for applying rules	KS2
Praising children's spontaneous use of grammatical rules	KS1 + 2

PROGRESSION IN KNOWLEDGE OF DIFFERENT COUNTRIES, CULTURES AND PEOPLE

Establishing contact with a partner school abroad	KS1 + 2
Using authentic material to bring the culture alive	KS1 + 2
Making comparisons with children's own culture and discussing our multicultural society	KS2
Making contact with native speakers of other languages	KS2

From age 7 onwards, when children's mother-tongue skills and confidence are increasing, it should be possible to expose them gradually to all four language skills: Listening, Speaking, Reading, Writing. Clearly, Listening and Speaking remain paramount, but slowly we should help children to progress from reading single words and captions to speech bubbles of simple dialogue in short sentences, questions and answers, for example:

> *Bonjour Monsieur. C'est combien ce nounours, s'il vous plaît?*
> *Ça fait 10 euros 50.*
> *Et ce livre d'aventures?*
> *Ça fait 12 euros 10.*
> *Voilà. Merci et au revoir.*

There can be a clear progression here from word to sentence to text level in the course of language lessons at KS2.

WRITING

When you feel that your class is ready, copywriting should not be neglected. It will prove an added challenge and a useful aid for the children to record what they have already mastered orally. While writing can eat away at precious classroom time, children can be encouraged, towards the end of a lesson, to attempt simple writing tasks which they can finish at home. Many European countries introduce copywriting at an early age and encourage children to look at spellings carefully, providing exercises in matching halves of words or sentences, sequencing sentences, filling in missing letters of words, or the missing words in sentences and stories, all of which reinforce the work of the Literacy Strategy.

> *Remets les mots dans le bon ordre:*

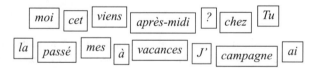

Another advantage of introducing copywriting is that children can begin to assemble the language items and phrases they have learnt in their own foreign language dossier/Portfolio. This could be a list of illustrated vocabulary by topic (i.e. a homemade picture dictionary, built up during the year) or a collection of phrases or sentences, demonstrating that 'This is what I know and can say in … [language]'.

READING

As your class develops its reading skills, the children can be introduced to simple picture dictionaries (ELI, Usborne) where they can be set simple tasks to learn dictionary skills (listing words alphabetically by initial letter, then by the first two letters, etc, e.g. *bon, beurre, baguette, blouson, ballon …*).

They will of course enjoy most looking up the words that **they** want to know for their own use – and they are bound to ask you for foreign words that you don't know either! ('What's a stick insect in French?', 'How do you say: "My cat's just had three kittens …?" ')

These reference skills can be expanded throughout KS2 so that by Year 6 pupils will eventually be able to read and decipher authentic e-mails from your partner school abroad or look for information on selected foreign websites.

At KS2 there is scope to develop pairwork and groupwork – co-operative learning that leads to mutual help and lots of performance in the target language in role play, drama and story-telling. At this stage we would also expect pupils to be presented with an increasing range of listening material – listening to native speakers on audio-/videocassettes and listening to real people in class in the shape of Foreign Language Assistants, visiting trainee teachers from abroad or native speakers from the local community. Young Pathfinder 12: *Working together: Native speakers in the primary school* (Martin and Farren 2004) explores this in detail.

There should also be scope for increasing the challenge of the texts and the tasks that pupils encounter – progressing from simple dialogues to longer texts, short stories and fairy tales. Children should be encouraged to read for information and for pleasure in the foreign language as well as in English, as this is a vital skill for their adult lives; see, for example, Mary Glasgow Magazines and ELI Magazines in four languages and easy readers in the European Schoolbooks catalogue.

You will find a range of excellent ideas about phasing in reading and writing skills in Young Pathfinder 5: *First steps to reading and writing* (Skarbek 1998) and in Young Pathfinder 9: *The literacy link* (Cheater and Farren 2001).

 ## GRAMMAR

There is no reason why KS2 pupils should not be equipped to cope with basic grammatical concepts, as Lydia Biriotti demonstrates in Young Pathfinder 8: *Grammar is fun* (1999) and the accompanying CILT ResourceFile 3: *Getting the basics right* (2001).

We have a lot of groundwork done for us now in the Literacy Strategy, so you need not hesitate to enter into simple explanations of how language works and how every language has certain rules and patterns. You will need to explain the concept of gender at an early stage in every European language, so children should be encouraged to collect nouns in their dossier or in a class dictionary box by colour-coding masculine/feminine (neuter) from the beginning. They also need to understand singular/plural in personal pronouns, and the plural of nouns is unavoidable, though probably best kept low-key at primary level, especially if you teach German!

Children will also want to use tenses in natural conversation. When talking about their pets, for example, they may want to say:

J'ai un lapin. J'avais un chien ... mais il est mort.
Je voudrais bien ... un petit chaton.

Ich habe ein Kaninchen. Ich hatte einen Hund ... aber er ist gestorben.
Ich hätte gern ... ein kleines Kätzchen.

Tengo un conejo. Tenía un perro ... pero murío.
De verdad que me gustaría tener un gatito.

As David Hicks demonstrates in the CILT Early Language Learning video 3: *Making it better*, tenses can be practised very naturally in the everyday class discussion of recent events and intentions in the immediate future:

Qu'est-ce que tu fais aujourd'hui? Qu'est-ce que tu as fais hier/lundi?
Qu'est-ce que tu vas faire demain/dimanche?

Was machst du heute? Was hast du gestern/am Montag gemacht?
Was machst du morgen/am Sonntag?

Qué haces hay? ¿Qué hiciste ayer/lunes?
¿Qué vas hacer mañana/domingo?

Children's answers could be:

J'ai joué ... au foot/au tennis.
J'ai fait du ... vélo/du skate.

Ich habe ... Fußball/Tennis gespielt.
Ich war im Stadion/in der Stadt/im Park.

Jugué al fútbol/al tenis.
Hice ciclismo/fui a patinar.

Children will enjoy telling what they have been doing at the weekend/on holidays, so we cannot avoid past tenses, even if we wanted to – and primary pupils are quite capable of handling set phrases such as:

Où est-tu allé ... samedi soir?
Je suis allé ... à Londres/au club/chez mes amis.
J'étais ... chez Mémé et Pépé/chez ma tante Louise.

Wo warst du am Samstag?
Ich war ... in London/im Jugendklub/bei meinen Freunden.
Ich war ... bei Oma und Opa/bei Tante Luise.

¿Adónde fuiste sábado?
Fui ... a Londres/al club juvenil/a la casa de mis amigos.

Ultimately we should be aiming to equip our learners, before they leave primary school, with the skills to access information about the culture of the countries where the language is spoken. They should be able to read simple authentic texts from foreign magazines that interest them; and they should be made aware that French is spoken in over 40 countries across the world, not just in France; that Spanish is the language of Mexico and much of South America; that German is spoken in Austria, Switzerland and Luxembourg, as well as in Germany …

We also need to raise awareness of the culture and customs of the countries – that we may have many things in common, but that there are significant differences in customs and behaviour from one country to another. If people speak a different language they often **think** a different language. Language and culture are inseparable. Even in the earliest stages of language learning children will encounter new ways of greeting people – which formulae do you use to greet children, which to adults (*Vous/tu, Sie/du, Usted/tú* …) or when do you shake hands in France/Germany/Austria? All of which is part and parcel of the culture and inextricably woven into the language.

You will find the videos produced by Early Start Languages and by KETV are really excellent for transporting your learners of French, Spanish or German straight into the culture of the countries concerned, so that they can see and hear the language they are learning in class being used in real life: families at breakfast, children in school, going shopping, pursuing their hobbies and looking after their pets.

If possible, we should take our Year 6 classes on their first brief visit abroad to practise what they have learnt in class – even if it is only three days to Calais or Normandy. We need to reinforce the fact that everyone in France speaks French all day every day! But such visits need to be carefully planned and structured to ensure that all pupils get the most out of the trip and really have to use some foreign language while there. The short handbook *Fieldwork in action 6: Crossing the channel* (ed. May and Richardson 1998) is full of useful ideas to help plan a trip abroad and includes examples of cross-curricular activities for children of primary school age.

You will also find useful information on finding partner schools abroad on the British Council's Global Gateway website (**www.globalgateway.org.uk**).

MEASURING AND RECORDING PROGRESS

For many primary school teachers and, indeed, pupils the joy of learning a language is that it is one of the few curriculum areas that is not formally assessed. There are thankfully no SATS in foreign languages at KS1 or KS2. Many Year 6 class teachers in particular have often expressed their feeling that one of the reasons their pupils enjoy their foreign language lessons so much is because they are a 'light relief' from the pressures they are facing in other curriculum areas. (This same point was made to us by Franz Schimek in 1997 when describing the experience of piloting the primary English scheme in Vienna in the early 1990s: the foreign language was the only subject not formally tested and therefore received with enthusiasm by teachers, pupils and parents.)

Although some headteachers are concerned about fitting a foreign language into their KS2 timetable, others acknowledge that it brings so much to their pupils in terms of active learning and developing other skills, that they are very creative in finding space for the subject. We are not saying that pupils should not be assessed at all, but we do believe in teachers' professional skill in informally assessing their pupils.

Teachers therefore need to build into their planning some method of measuring their pupils' progress. The *NACELL best practice guide* has a useful section on Assessment and Recording which we would recommend to primary teachers, as links are made between the QCA Scheme of Work and the Teacher's Guide for languages at KS2 and the new Language Learning Ladder – the National Recognition Scheme to be launched in 2005 (see p33). Here it is suggested that the first four National Curriculum attainment targets for Modern Foreign Languages can be applied to KS2. The first four level descriptions for each Attainment Target are also included in the non-statutory Guidelines for Foreign Languages at KS2.

They are included to inform planning when evaluating children's progress and may also be used when transferring information from class to class and from school to school.

At KS3, where a foreign language is statutory, equal weighting is given to all four skills: Listening, Speaking, Reading, Writing. But at KS2, although pupils will be working in all four skill areas, there will not be equal weighting. At KS1, we would expect the emphasis to be different again: although, as we have said above, the youngest pupils should not be denied the opportunity to read and write simple words/phrases in the foreign language, we would expect the emphasis to be predominantly on listening and speaking activities.

At the time of writing there is limited evidence and guidance about assessment at KS1. However, there is a particularly helpful case study from the DfES Best Practice Research Project. A Kent primary teacher, Tara Deevoy, found that teacher observation and assessment activities which were built into the lesson were the most efficient. She used teaching activities requiring a physical response with her younger pupils and verbal or written activities with the older pupils. A summary of her findings can be found on the *NACELL best practice guide, 'Assessment and recording'*.

This website also provides some examples of very useful and practical assessment sheets for Reception, Years 1 and 2 (reproduced at the end of this chapter) which would form an excellent lead-in to recording progress with the *European Language Portfolio* (see overleaf).

You will also find some useful self-assessment sheets as part of published course materials, for example in the KETV and Early Start *French/Spanish/German* materials.

EUROPEAN LANGUAGE PORTFOLIO

The *European Language Portfolio* was developed and piloted by the Council of Europe and many member states introduced it in 2001, the European Year of Languages. In the UK CILT organised and evaluated pilots of the junior and adult versions, and the junior model was trialled in several LEAs and independent schools across England before publication in 2001.

The purpose of the Portfolio is to record a child's experience of all languages. This means it may include experiences and achievements in foreign language learning and mother-tongue learning.

The Portfolio belongs to the learner and states clearly that 'This Portfolio is for you':

- *to show what you know and what you can do in languages;*
- *to help you see that you are making progress;*
- *to keep a record of your work in languages;*
- *to put some examples of work you've done in languages (these could be pictures, written work, speaking recorded on audio or video tape, homework);*
- *to show your new teachers when you move class or school.*

The Portfolio is a means of celebrating language-learning experiences, an open-ended record of achievement in languages and a valuable source of information to aid transfer to the next class or school. During the piloting it was revealing to discover how many other languages the children spoke at home and this gave a real opportunity to value their knowledge.

The Portfolio contains a **'Languages passport'** in which the children record their language-learning experiences – and this may require some help from parents.

The children should be encouraged to include any language-learning clubs, contacts with native speakers or visits that have helped them to develop their knowledge and understanding of different languages and countries. Teachers may also wish to include an outline of the language-learning programme in their school.

The **'Language biography'** takes the form of a personalised learning diary, listing specific achievements in each of the four skill areas. Speech bubbles are provided for the children to colour in when they are able to complete a given task: 'I can say a rhyme', for example. In our experience the children really enjoy this and are incredibly honest and hard on themselves! Some teachers use similar pages from their own resource files. *Early Start French* has some examples.

'Getting better' is a self-assessment section which allows the children to evaluate their own competence. The statements provided are based on the level descriptors in the National Curriculum for Modern Foreign Languages. An indication is also given of how these levels might correspond to those defined in the *Common European Framework for Language Learning*

(Council of Europe 1996). Teachers may find these sheets useful at the end of the school year when children move classes or school.

'My dossier' is a record of children's work. The pupil chooses what goes into this section, whether it is classwork, homework, creative, written or spoken work. The children in the pilot were very positive about the dossier which is like a 'Good work folder'. Some primary schools keep all the children's work in the Portfolio and make their selection at the end of the year, like a Record of Achievement.

The Portfolio is available in a loose-leaf format from CILT together with a separate Teacher's Guide, which shows how to use the Portfolio and how the can-do statements link in both to the National Curriculum levels and the Common European Framework. It can also be downloaded from the NACELL website: **www.nacell.org.uk/elp.htm.** You can also inspect it at Comenius Centres and in the CILT Resources Library.

The Portfolio will be compatible with the new National Recognition System and will provide a vital tool for teachers and pupils to track progress up the Languages Ladder.

It is already proving a valuable transfer document between primary and secondary schools and we quote below from a report by Hazel Brent at Ryton Comprehensive School in Tyne and Wear:

'Un monstre', selected by a pupil for her dossier

We decided two years ago to invest in the European Languages Portfolio *for all our Year 6 pupils as we viewed it as being an ideal tool to record and celebrate success, achievement and progression. The experiment has proved successful, so much so that we plan to extend a similar scheme through KS3 and 4.*

Advantages

- *The Year 6 pupils respond very positively to the Portfolio. Those with mother-tongue competence in another language are pleased and proud to see this recognised.*
- *Virtually every lesson gives us the opportunity to colour in another speech bubble, or tick off another skill. With such small steps even the least able can see progress. The Portfolio is hugely motivating.*
- *The Portfolio offers a very stylish, professional format which the pupils respect.*

- *It can be used to store 'special' pieces of work, and as such encourages attention to detail and presentation, or such items as song lyrics, poems and posters.*
- *At the point of transfer to KS3 these pupil-friendly methods of recording progress by self- and peer-assessment enable staff to gauge relative levels of attainment. We have thus found a credible alternative to formal tests on entry to Year 7.*
- *Finally, the Portfolio is of such high quality in production terms that even the most reluctant pupil tends to be loath to put in substandard work.*

THE NEW LANGUAGES LADDER – THE NATIONAL RECOGNITION SCHEME FOR LANGUAGES

The idea of the scheme as set out in the *National Languages Strategy* (2001) is 'to complement existing qualification frameworks and give people credit for their language skills'. The Ladder is made up of six stages, each subdivided into grades, as set out below.

THE LANGUAGES LADDER

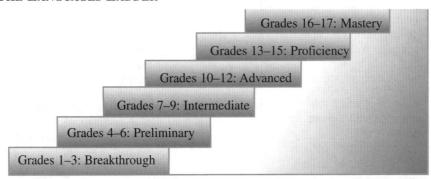

As far as primary pupils are concerned, teachers will be concerned principally with the first stage, **Breakthrough**, which will consist of three steps: Grades 1–3. It is clear that most children will be able to achieve Grade 3 easily before they reach the end of KS2 – and many may well progress to the **Preliminary stage:** Grades 4–6. This will be revealed once the Ladder is in place and the children have shown us just how far they can climb at primary school!

Each of the language skills may be assessed discretely. The level of performance in each is defined by 'can do' statements as set out in the tables below. Learners are not expected to be at the same grade in each skill, so do not need to complete one grade in all skills before moving on.

Breakthrough: Grade 1	
Listening	I can understand a few familiar spoken words and phrases.
Speaking	I can say/repeat a few words and short simple phrases.
Reading	I can recognise and read out a few familiar words and phrases.
Writing	I can write or copy simple words or symbols.

Breakthrough: Grade 2	
Listening	I can understand a range of familiar spoken phrases.
Speaking	I can answer simple questions and give basic information.
Reading	I can understand familiar written phrases.
Writing	I can write one or two short sentences and fill the words in on a simple form.

Breakthrough: Grade 3

Listening	I can understand the main point(s) from a short spoken message.
Speaking	I can ask and answer simple questions and talk about my interests.
Reading	I can understand the main point(s) from a short written passage in clear printed script.
Writing	I can write 2–3 short sentences, using reference materials/with the support of a peer.

Preliminary: Grade 4

Listening	I can understand the main points and some of the detail from a short spoken passage.
Speaking	I can take part in a simple conversation and I can express my opinions.
Reading	I can understand the main points and some of the detail from a short written passage.
Writing	I can write a short passage of 3–4 sentences, using reference materials/with the support of a peer.

Preliminary: Grade 5

Listening	I can understand the main points and simple opinions (e.g. likes and dislikes) of a longer spoken passage.
Speaking	I can give a short prepared talk, on a topic of my choice, including expressing my opinions.
Reading	I can understand the main points and simple opinions (e.g. likes and dislikes) of a longer written passage.
Writing	I can write a short passage on everyday topics.

Preliminary: Grade 6

Listening	I can understand spoken passages referring to past or future events.
Speaking	I can give a short prepared talk, on a topic of my choice expressing opinions and answering simple questions about it.
Reading	I can understand longer passages and distinguish present and past or future events.
Writing	I can write a simple text, e.g. a letter, giving and seeking information.

François Hall

We must make clear that these assessments are voluntary and are intended to be used flexibly and offered to the learners whenever they and the teacher think they are ready. Please note that at the time of writing, the National Recognition Scheme is in a development phase, with the first external assessments available in 2005/06. For further information, please see **www.dfes.gov.uk/ languages/DSP_languagesladder.cfm**.

As we have said above, all of these achievements can and should be recorded in the children's Languages Portfolio. In time, the Portfolio will gain international recognition across Europe and become part of an adult 'Languages Passport', which, when added to a CV in applications for jobs that require language skills, should prove of real interest to employers.

PRIMARY–SECONDARY LIAISON

One of the most important issues in early language learning is that of transition and ensuring progression from primary to secondary schools. In the *National Languages Strategy* it is emphasised that transition arrangements must be improved if achievement is to be recognised and enthusiasm sustained. Happily, over the years since the first edition of this book was published there appears to be much evidence of primary and secondary schools working closer together than ever before. In part this is thanks to such initiatives as the DfEE/CILT Good Practice Project and the advent of Specialist Language Colleges.

At a local level, primary schools need to work together in clusters or families of schools to share planning, best practice and professional development. Equally, they need to work with secondary schools to share information about curriculum planning and pupil achievement. In authorities where Advisory Staff are still employed, one of their most important roles is to organise liaison meetings. This can also be done by the Languages department in secondary schools or Specialist Language Colleges.

The Good Practice Project co-ordinated by CILT involved Local Education Authorities, clusters of primary schools with their partner secondary school or Specialist Language College and individual primary schools. This project identified examples of effective liaison, some of which are outlined below.

- Year 6 pupils spend a day at their local secondary school and demonstrate what they have learnt, for example groups perform songs they have learnt.
- Use of the *European Language Portfolio* to record achievement and progress. It can be used to transfer information when a pupil changes class or moves to secondary school.

- LEA organises a European Day for all Year 6 pupils, allowing them to demonstrate what they have learnt, staffed by both primary and secondary school teachers.
- MFL joint meetings for primary and secondary schools, held once a term, for planning and exchange of information.
- LEA circulates MFL newsletter covering both primary and secondary issues.
- Specialist Language Colleges offer places within their own adult or community education classes in foreign languages to all staff from primary schools, teaching and non-teaching. There is usually no charge for these classes.
- Shared use of the Foreign Language Assistant.
- Reciprocal visits to observe lessons.
- Shared events; International Days or weeks, including the European Day of Languages (26 September).
- Joint INSET.

The *NACELL best practice guide* also gives ideas for ensuring smooth transition to secondary, including the following:

- guidance on transition – Richmond upon Thames LEA;
- planning for continuity and progression: a bridging unit for Years 6–7 – South Gloucestershire LEA;
- using the *European Language Portfolio* – Liverpool Education and Lifelong Learning Service; Richmond upon Thames LEA.

Another useful source of information about liaison is the QCA Scheme of Work (**www.standards. dfes.gov.uk/schemes/primary_mfl/?view=get**) which outlines a bridging topic, designed to be taught at the end of Year 6 and into Year 7. Unit 12: *'Un pays francophone'* allows primary children to consolidate and celebrate what they have already learnt. This could be built on by the receiving secondary school in a variety of ways. Perhaps a display of the work done in the primary school could be put up, ready to 'welcome' the new Year 7 pupils.

The sample assessment sheets reproduced opposite show how aspects of the QCA Scheme of work can be assessed simply and in an encouraging way for learners.

The issues of primary-secondary transfer and teacher liaison are dealt with in great detail by Ann Gregory and Rosemary Bevis in CILT Young Pathfinder 13: *Mind the Gap!* (2006). This book suggests a wide range of ideas for cooperation and teamwork between groups of primary schools and their local secondary language departments.

From *NACELL best practice guide*
'Assessment and recording',
'Examples of assessment sheets' – DfES
Best Practice Research Project, Kent

Assessment sheet Year R

Areas planned	Areas taught	☺	Assessment comments
Know how to say 'hello' and 'goodbye'			
Know how to sing 'Happy birthday'			
Know how to say 'thank you'			
Know some words for people in your family			
Know some words for pets			
Know some words for parts of the body			
Know some words for clothes			
Know how to ask for an ice cream			
Know how to say what the weather is like			
Know some words for things you might find in class			
Know your numbers from 1–10			
Know the alphabet song			
Know some colours			
Know the days of the week			

Assessment sheet Year 1

Areas planned	Areas taught	☺	Assessment comments
Know how to ask how someone is and say how you are			
Know how to ask what someone's name is and say what yours is			
Know how to ask how old someone is and say how old you are			
Know how to ask where someone lives and say where you live			
Know how to ask who someone is and answer			
Know some more words for pets			
Know some more words for parts of the body			
Know some more words for clothes			
Know how to ask for a sandwich and crisps.			
Know how to ask what the weather is like			
Know some words for school subjects			
Know your numbers from 11–20			
Know your vowels			
Know some more colours			
Know the months of the year			

Assessment sheet Year 2

Areas planned	Areas taught	☺	Assessment comments
Know some more greetings			
Know how to ask when someone's birthday is and say when yours is			
Know how to ask if someone has brothers and sisters and say if you have			
Know how to ask if someone has pets and say if you have			
Know how to say that your head, etc hurts			
Know how to ask what someone is wearing and say what you are wearing			
Know how to ask for a drink			
Know how to ask what the weather is like in Folkestone and answer			
Know how to ask what subject someone likes and say what you like/dislike			
Know your numbers from 21–31			
Know how to spell your name			
Know how to ask what colour something is and answer			
Know how to ask what the date is and answer			

3. Methods and activities that work ... and still work

Although there have been many developments in the field of early language learning, those methods and activities outlined as 'good practice' in Young Pathfinder 1: *Catching them young* (1995), remain an integral part of our classroom methodology and stand the test of time. Even though many of these activities are familiar to those of us who have been involved in primary languages for some time, for those people who are teaching a foreign language for the first time, it is worth outlining activities that have worked for us.

 ## GAMES

FLASHCARD GAMES

- 'Guess the card'
- 'Repeat if it is true'
- 'Noughts and crosses'
- 'Touch the flashcard'

NUMBER GAMES

- 'Lotto': although this is a very popular and well-used game there are variations and practical ways to enhance the experience. The quickest way to produce a lotto grid is to use a noughts and crosses design.

  Another variation is to ask pupils to draw four lotto grids and fill in one of the grids with any four numbers between nought and fifteen, for example. The pupils take it in turns to call out a number while the teacher keeps track on a piece of paper.

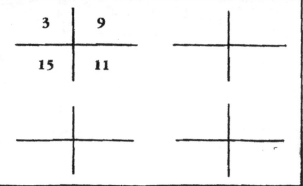

- Continue until one pupil has all four numbers crossed out and calls out *'Ça y est!'* or another phrase perhaps, *'J'ai gagné!'*. That pupil then reads back the winning numbers and if they are correct, he or she wins. Vary again by asking a pupil to read all four numbers in a grid. Any other pupil with an identical grid wins.

To save time, a lotto grid, which has been prepared and photocopied, can be useful (see example right).

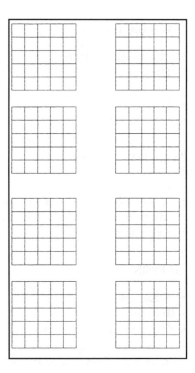

- *'Effacez!'*: The class is divided into two teams and a selection of numbers to be practised is written on the board in a random fashion. One member of each team comes to the board and the teacher calls out a number. The first team member to rub out the correct number gains a point for his or her team. Pupils can also take the teacher's role and call out the numbers. Other versions of this game involve having numbers written on the board which have to be circled

according to the teacher's instructions or having a blank board and pupils have to write the number that has been called out. This activity also works well with letters of the alphabet.

- *'Plouf!'*: The numbers which are to be practised are written on the board in the form of stepping-stones across a river. To cross the river safely, the numbers have to be said correctly. If an error is made the pupil 'falls' in the water.

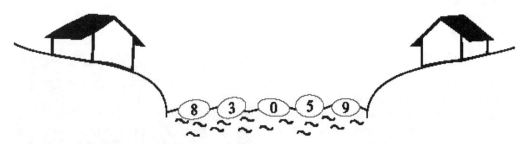

- 'Beetle' and other dice games
- 'Fizz, buzz'
- mental Maths – mini-whiteboards are very useful

CARD GAMES

- 'Pelmanism' or 'Pairs'
- 'Dominoes'
- 'Snap'
- 'Happy families'
- flashcard games

MEMORY GAMES

- 'Kim's game'
- sequencing – this is a variation on 'Kim's game'. Objects are shown in a sequence and pupils have to be able to say them in the correct order
- 'I went to market and I bought ...'

GUESSING GAMES

- 'What is in the bag?'
- 'Hangman'
- 'Hide and seek' with objects
- lip reading for specific words
- drawing numbers, letters or words on someone's back

BOARD GAMES

- 'Snakes and ladders'
- homemade games

ACTIVE GAMES

- 'Simon says'
- 'Fruit salad': pupils are given the name of a fruit; four or five different ones work well. The teacher calls out 'lemons' and all the lemons change places. If 'fruit salad' is called, everyone changes. This can also be played with chairs and with the added excitement of removing one chair after each go!
- 'Show me ...' and 'Bring me ...'
- miming

These games are explained in some in detail in Young Pathfinder 2: *Games and fun activities* (Martin 1995), but there are some others that we have discovered and which have become part of our repertoire. They include:

- 'Pictogram': This game can be played in teams or groups to practise new vocabulary and requires reading and understanding. The target words are written on cards. Postcards work well for this. The topic could be pets, for

une Souris

example. A volunteer comes to the board and selects a card, at random, from the pack. If they have 'une souris' written on the card they have to draw the given pet on the board and the other team has to guess what the animal may be. Points are awarded. This game works well with a wide range of topics, including sports and clothes.

- Name game: A volunteer comes to the board and turns his or her back to the class, covering his or her eyes with their hands. He or she asks the question, in the target language, 'What's your name?'. The teacher selects a volunteer who answers 'My name is [Bart Simpson]', at the same time disguising the sound of his or her voice. If the pupil at the front guesses correctly who has spoken, he or she stays at the front, if wrong he or she changes places.

- 'Number/alphabet tennis': This is a very simple means to practise numbers and letters. Instead of hitting a ball back and forth between two players, pupils bat the numbers or letters to each other. If someone 'miss hits', he or she starts again. If more competition is wanted, play against the clock.

- 'Secret code': This is another means of practising the numbers 1–26 and the alphabet, at a slightly higher level. The pupils are given a sheet with the alphabet and a number next to each letter. Therefore, A = 1, B = 2, C = 3 and so on. The teacher selects a word and calls out the appropriate numbers. '6, 15, 15, 20, 2, 1, 12, 12' equals 'football'.

A	1	H	8	O	15	V	22
B	2	I	9	P	16	W	23
C	3	J	10	Q	17	X	24
D	4	K	11	R	18	Y	25
E	5	L	12	S	19	Z	26
F	6	M	13	T	20		
G	7	N	14	U	21		

- 'Les noms': This game can be used to reinforce the alphabet. Call out a letter and then call out the pupils' names beginning with that letter. Raise your hands to indicate that these pupils should stand up. Once the pupils understand the game, call out a letter and when the pupils stand up, ask them to say their name.

SONGS AND MUSIC

Most primary school teachers are already skilled at delivering music as part of the curriculum, but why not use music when teaching a foreign language? Pupils will often be more relaxed and as the whole class sings, every child can be involved and there is less pressure on individuals. Pupils who may have some difficulty remembering taught language, will often have no problem when producing a phrase as part of a song. Above all, songs are fun, motivating and can be exploited in a variety of ways.

Cynthia Martin has written ResourceFile 6: *Rhythm and rhyme – Developing language in French and German* (2002), which links to Young Pathfinder 6: *Let's join in* (1998), written with Catherine Cheater. These publications offer practical support to specialist and non-specialist primary language teachers.

However, not all teachers are confident about singing in front of a class, myself included! Nevertheless, over the past few years, music has played a much greater part in my lessons and has often transformed them. Some units in my programme of work even have a song as their starting point. How has this transformation happened? Firstly, there have been some excellent CDs that have come on to the market which I am more than happy to sing along to, and so are my classes. Secondly, I have been lucky enough to attend some inspirational in-service training sessions led by David Hicks, an Advanced Skills Teacher and the Primary French Co-ordinator at Impington Village Language College, Cambridgeshire. He uses mime, rhythm and music as a focus for his lessons. He has recorded a CD: *Les chansons et les raps de Monsieur X.* Thirdly, I have worked with some brilliant music teachers who have been only too glad to incorporate French into their lessons.

How can music and song be used?:

- to present new vocabulary and structures;
- for mime;
- to listen for detail;
- to listen and respond physically;
- as part of an assembly or a performance;
- to record on video or audiocassette;
- to exchange songs with link schools.

One of the CDs I have found the most useful is *1, 2, 3 soleil!* (Husar 1997) and one of the most popular tracks with my pupils is *'Léon le caméléon'*. This can be exploited in many of the ways listed above and on several different levels. If you wish to practise the vocabulary for colours, for example, give pupils coloured blocks and ask them to hold them up every time 'their' colour is mentioned. They can respond in a similar way with flashcards, or by standing up or raising a thumb each time the appropriate word is heard. At a higher level, this song lends itself very well to a cloze exercise. Some classes have simply enjoyed illustrating the song (for example see right) and several pupils have chosen work related to this to include in the best work section of their *European Language Portfolio.*

Many teachers are able to write their own tunes or songs to practise and reinforce vocabulary, however another strategy is to ask the pupils to set new words to a familiar melody of their choice. The refrain for *'Frère Jacques'*, for example, lends itself very well to practising the days of the week in French. Another teacher uses the tune of 'London's burning' to practise the days of the week in German.

Léon, le caméléon

At KS1 songs and music can form the basis of all lessons. 'Head, shoulders, knees and toes' can provide weeks of work through actions, new vocabulary and, of course, singing.

RAPS AND RHYMES

Producing raps, writing poems and practising simple rhymes are motivating and enjoyable activities in a very similar way to songs. In recent years, I have included the introduction of the French alphabet to my programme of work. Knowledge of the alphabet is one of the learning objectives of the Literacy Strategy. In Young Pathfinder 9: *The literacy link* (Cheater and Farren 2001), they give several very useful activities involving the letters.

As well as the resources mentioned in Young Pathfinder 9: *The literacy link*, I have found two CDs by Bruno Husar that are excellent for alphabet work. Firstly, for introducing or practising the alphabet, *'Rapalphabet'*, which can also be found on the *1, 2, 3 soleil!* CD and has an instrumental version which provides an enjoyable opportunity for some karaoke! Secondly, *'Alphabet techno'* from the *1, 2, 3, techno* CD, provides an excellent opportunity for some cross-curricular work involving atlases, for example.

Poetry can be used in many different ways. With some help, pupils can create original 'poems'. The poems can be simply two-line rhyming couplets.

Bonne fête,	*Ich bin cool/stark/frei*	*¡Buenos días!*
Mariette.	*Bist du cool?*	*¡Amigas mías!*
Bravo!	*Ja, logo, ja!*	*Contámos a cien*
Il fait beau.	*Wunderbar!*	*¡Qué bien!*
	Alles klar!	
De quelle couleur,		
Est l'ordinateur?	*Dankeschön!*	
	Wiedersehen!	

Of course, poetry doesn't have to rhyme and ideas for producing shape and acrostic poems, for example, can be found in many primary school poetry books.

There are several ways in which this activity can be set up:

- make lists of rhyming words with the help of the class and write on the OHP/board;
- give pairs or groups of pupils a sound. They make up a list of words ending with that sound. Again record as above.

Once you have a list of rhyming words the pupils can create simple poems, working in pairs or small groups. These can be made into a display using ICT or become part of a class poetry book.

There are many excellent poems already in the primary classroom and these can be adapted successfully into the foreign language.

Tongue twisters can be practised at different speeds and with differing intonation as well as being fun. Pupils can try creating their own tongue twisters, e.g. *'Le cochon cache son cornichon dans la chambre'* and *'Sept souris sont sous son sac'*.

Counting and nonsense rhymes, such as *'Am, stram, gram'*, provide another useful means to practise intonation and to enjoy the sounds of another language.

 ## GROUP ACTIVITIES

The very nature of language is social. Therefore, small group, partner work and co-operative activities play an extremely important part in learning a foreign language. What are the advantages of group work?

- It provides variety.
- It encourages pupils to work independently using their new language.
- It usually requires co-operation among the pupils to complete a task.
- Pupils are motivated to use the language in a meaningful way.

Primary practitioners are experienced in the organisation of groupings within the primary classroom and can easily use this skill in the foreign language lesson. Most of the activities already mentioned in this chapter are suitable for group work. Others include:

DRAMA-BASED ACTIVITIES

- role play
- dialogues
- producing a playlet
- scripting a playlet
- puppet plays
- miming

The most popular scenes among pupils usually take place in a café or restaurant, in a market or shop, at a fashion show, giving the weather report on television, or being a contestant on 'Blind Date'. Pupils also enjoy taking on a character too; they can become someone famous, an alien or someone entirely of their own creation. Be prepared for boys trying to include a fight or a fall in their performances!

PRACTICAL ACTIVITIES

These can be very successful when carried out in groups.

- Carrying out surveys and recording and displaying the results.
- Designing posters.
- Producing a display.

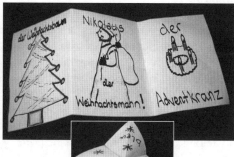

- Cooking.
- Making models, books, dice, spinners, games, mobiles, fortune-tellers.

SOFT TOYS AND PUPPETS

We talked fairly briefly about puppets in Young Pathfinder 1: *Catching them young* and since returning to the primary classroom and becoming a parent, my use of soft toys, in particular, has increased considerably. Although soft toys and puppets are ideal for use in pre-school and at KS1, they are still popular with older pupils. They can be used in a variety of ways:

- to play 'What's in the bag?';
- to initiate language;
- to produce dialogues and plays;
- to use as a model for repetition;
- to show how to play games;
- to bring a second foreign language speaker into the room;
- to be the characters when telling stories in the target language.

Most primary schools already have a stock of puppets and soft toys; they can also provide the catalogues should you need to order them. Finger puppets are available commercially, Ikea, for example sell a lovely set of animal finger puppets for £5. If you are a parent, raid the toy box, and children always enjoy the opportunity to bring in their own soft toys! Sponge or knitted dice, soft balls or beanbags are equally useful when wanting to initiate language. As well as soft toys, figures such as 'Action Man' or 'Barbie' can be used to great effect in a variety of ways; when teaching clothes vocabulary, for example.

Pupils can, of course make their own puppets, and this practical activity can be carried out in the target language. Puppets can be made in the following ways:

- using an old sock;
- from a paper bag;
- with a paper plate on a stick;
- paper finger puppets;
- from an A5 brown envelope;
- sewn from felt;
- using old gloves.

STORYTELLING

Telling simple stories in the target language remains an enjoyable and motivating way to develop pupils' skills. Listening to a story obviously helps to develop this skill but also the value of listening simply for pleasure should not be forgotten. Since Young Pathfinder 1: *Catching them young*, many excellent publications have been produced which provide guidelines on story telling in the primary school. Young Pathfinder 3: *Are you sitting comfortably?* (Tierney and Dobson 1995) is particularly helpful in detailing the type of stories that work well and the different ways a story can be presented. The book also gives ideas for following up a story and makes suggestions as to how story telling can be integrated into the primary curriculum.

Young Pathfinder 9: *The literacy link* outlines how a foreign language can be integrated into the primary school day and enhance literacy development. The authors explain how listening to stories is an element of text-level work that contributes greatly to young learners' language development. Recreating stories gives pupils another opportunity to work with and manipulate text.

Story telling through pictures (Dobson et al 1998) provides a useful set of resources for teachers who are wanting to use story telling in their classroom and would be suitable for 8 to 11 year-old pupils. There is also an introduction to story telling in the MLG publication *Ici on parle français* (also available in German and Spanish versions). This is a flexible resource which offers support to non-specialist teachers of languages who have some knowledge of the language.

Many Big Books that can be found in a KS1 classroom can be adapted to the foreign language simply by using Post-it notes to cover over and change the text. Many traditional stories like 'Goldilocks' can be found in Big Book format and their familiarity makes them popular with the pupils. Some other stories that are equally successful are:

- *The very hungry caterpillar* (Carle 1970);
- *Mr Gumpy's outing* (Burningham 1970);
- *The enormous turnip;*
- *The three little pigs;*
- *Little Red Riding Hood.*

ICT

In the *National Languages Strategy* the importance of and the need to maximise the potential of ICT is stressed throughout. Although the use of ICT in schools is growing, it is underdeveloped in over three quarters of primary schools. Teachers need to harness the power of ICT to develop the ability of pupils, engage learners and provide access to a wider range of language experiences.

In the *National Languages Strategy* a considerable emphasis is placed on ways in which schools can use ICT and e-learning to teach languages. This is also echoed in the *NACELL best practice guide*. ICT can provide exposure to native speakers and it gives teaching opportunities that will engage many pupils, especially boys. Stand-alone e-learning materials can provide opportunities for practice, rehearsal and support for speaking, reading, listening and writing skills. By using the Internet, teachers have access to a range of resources, including websites, newspapers, radio and TV. Schools can communicate easily through e-mail and videoconferencing. One of the most successful aspects of ICT has been through e-pal links which involve exchange of information, materials and resources. Teachers wishing to find e-mail partners can consult: **www.nacell.org. uk/networking/schools_links.htm**.

It is not possible here to outline all the software materials and appropriate websites to enhance the teaching of early language learning, but a visit to the NACELL website will give you advice on choosing software and on which websites support teaching and learning of languages to young learners in many different languages. The *NACELL best practice guide* has a very helpful section on ICT which suggests that schools might investigate:

- interactive whiteboards;
- digital and video cameras;
- use of software such as PowerPoint;
- CD-ROMs.

Links to on-line resources for early language learning can be found at: **www.nacell.org.uk/ resources/online_resources.htm**. There are also some very useful case studies to be found in the ICT section of the *NACELL best practice guide*.

Helpful suggestions concerning the use of ICT are given by Catherine Cheater and Anne Farren in Young Patfinder 9: The literacy link (2001) and also in Young Pathfinder 14: We have the technology, (2007) in which Therese Comfort and Dan Tierney explore how teachers can use the Internet and the interactive whiteboard to enhance motivation, enliven story-telling and develop reading and writing skills.

Another useful point of reference for ICT work is the QCA Scheme of Work. For each unit of work, links with other subjects are given. For example, in Unit 4 where one of the learning objectives is that children should learn how others celebrate festivals, it is suggested that the children could use ICT to produce greetings cards. They would select and import appropriate images and combine them with text. They would use skills of centring, aligning and resizing graphics. Some would choose effects to match their purpose, ensuring that the text and graphics complement each other. They may be able to send their greetings by e-mail.

In Unit 10 the topic is 'Clothes' and again several opportunities are given for using ICT. Children with access to the Internet could explore some of the French shopping pages. They could then produce their own versions of the clothing adverts from the Internet pages.

While *Bringing it home* by Anne Farren and Richard Smith is aimed primarily at parents who wish to support their children's language learning, it also has some invaluable advice for teachers. This includes an excellent chapter on using the Internet. Throughout the book, the authors make references to show how the Internet can support children's foreign language learning but in Chapter 9, they give ideas of specific areas to look for and some useful websites.

REWARDS

There is nothing more motivating for learners than a sense of success. Building in a reward system as part of your programme of work is an important element of a positive learning experience. If pupils answer a question with an excellent accent or if they win a game, they can be rewarded with

a 'Bravo!' slip. These are easy to design on the computer. We have found these to be extremely popular and motivating for pupils of all abilities, as they reward effort, not just ability.

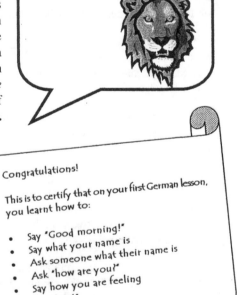

You can devise a system where three Bravo slips equates with a sticker; and for written and creative work you can award stamps – for creativity and/or accuracy. Three stamps are then worth a sticker; and ten stickers earn a certificate which can be given out in celebration assemblies – and included in the *European Language Portfolio* or in a similar document. A useful source of stickers, stamps and certificates is **www.superstickers. com**.

Class teachers may prefer to use their own reward systems, using merit, house or effort points. The important principle is not in testing the pupils but in **motivating** them.

Congratulations!

This is to certify that on your first German lesson, you learnt how to:

- Say "Good morning!"
- Say what your name is
- Ask someone what their name is
- Ask "how are you?"
- Say how you are feeling
- Say "bye!"

4. Teaching in the target language

 ## THE CURRENT SITUATION

In the 25–30% of English primary schools who already offer a foreign language the majority of teachers are generalist primary trained, not language specialists. Most have no formal language qualifications beyond, perhaps, a GCSE/O level or an A level.

This may not be an ideal baseline from which to start teaching the subject, but such teachers can, with appropriate classroom support and expert INSET provision, be brought to a threshold where they are competent and confident to teach one primary class for a year. This has been proven both in Scotland and in several English LEAs, notably Kent, Richmond upon Thames, Gloucestershire and Liverpool.

What we are saying is that you do not need to be a fluent languages graduate to teach German, French, Spanish or Italian in a primary school. The 400 plus primary teachers in Kent who have been twilight-trained over the past ten years with constant back-up from their Advisory Teacher are not fluent speakers and do not necessarily have marvellous accents, but they do have the confidence to teach a limited syllabus well (based round the video materials in *Pilote, Tú y yo*, and *3, 2, 1 … los!*).

If they can do it, so can many thousands more primary teachers, given time, encouragement, thorough training and continuing support from Advisory Teachers, Specialist Language College colleagues and Foreign Language Assistants.

In this chapter we will tackle briefly the key issues related to teaching in the target language in a primary classroom:

- Why use the target language?
- Can I do it?
- What do I need to know?
- What do the children need to learn?
- What sorts of language?
- Where can I get help?
- How much target language? How much English?
- Exposing children to the target language – listen, read, write.
- How should I plan my use of the target language?

You will find a much fuller discussion of the target language in Young Pathfinder 4: *Keep talking* (Satchwell 1997).

WHY USE THE TARGET LANGUAGE?

In contrast to our European neighbours where primary school children learning English as a foreign language are surrounded in their daily lives by English on TV, in pop songs, cartoons, advertising, sport and a welter of English products in shops and supermarkets, children in the UK are still, sadly, insulated from exposure to other European languages. Of their 4,000 plus waking hours per annum our children are cocooned almost exclusively in English. Your language lessons of perhaps 30–60 minutes a week add up to a mere 30–40 hours a year – if you are lucky!

This phenomenon was aptly described by Eric Hawkins (1987) as 'gardening in a gale', and although we now have more UK children who are linguistically aware, especially those bilingual pupils who are equally at home in their mother tongue and English, the majority rarely hear or see other languages in use outside your school classroom. For this reason alone it is important that we strive to make the most of the few minutes a week that we have to expose children to the foreign language – to cultivate that fragile foreign language 'flower' before the gale of English blows it flat the moment the children get outside your classroom door!

That does not mean that 100% of every lesson has to be taught in the target language. We must look, however, for cunning strategies to provide maximum exposure to the language – the spoken, sung and printed word – throughout the school week. Some teachers, for example, have found that by regularly playing a catchy song as the changeover signal for the foreign language lesson or as the class comes into the room, the children have quickly and subconsciously assimilated both tune and text without having spent much time practising it.

Other teachers display a 'phrase of the week' on the classroom wall:

> *Darf ich …   auf die Toilette gehen?*
> *hinausgehen?*
> *das Fenster aufmachen?*

> *Est-ce que je peux …   aller aux toilettes?*
> *sortir?*
> *ouvrir la fenêtre?*

> *¿Puedo …   ir al servicio?*
> *irme?*
> *abrir la ventana?*

which is then rehearsed at every opportunity.

CAN I DO IT?

You do not have to be a linguistic genius or a highly fluent speaker to teach effectively in the primary classroom. But you do need enthusiasm, confidence, a sense of fun, good organisation and above all a determination to improve your own knowledge of the language as you go – and not be afraid to make mistakes!

If you feel your French, German, Italian or Spanish is rusty and that you have never learnt the phrases you need to manage your class in the target language, there are now resources to help you. Make sure you have brushed up your skills **before** you embark on your scheme. You will in any case go on learning on the job, as we all do.

You do not need a huge repertoire: the motto is to keep it simple, to teach a small amount of language thoroughly, so that by the time your pupils transfer to secondary school they **know** what they know and can use it with confidence and enjoyment.

Here are some of the ways in which primary teachers have acquired enough language to teach it well for a year:

- For some years now LEAs such as Kent, Surrey, Richmond upon Thames, Gloucestershire, have been running INSET courses for primary teachers which combine training in methodology and linguistic refreshment in a limited number of topics. Find out whether your LEA offers any such INSET.
- In Liverpool the LEA has a policy of sending language experts – Advisory Teachers in French, German, Spanish – into classrooms to team teach with a Foreign Language Assistant, providing model lessons with the class teacher learning alongside the children, so that he or she can follow up and consolidate the work later in the week.
- In some areas where there are peripatetic language teachers, the visiting specialist may teach a lead lesson and then sit with the class teacher to prepare follow-up lessons to teach on his or her own.
- Some LEAs organise twilight courses that are topped up with a two-week course abroad, such as those run by CILT and the foreign embassies, where the teachers have the opportunity to learn more language and culture in context and to go into local primary schools and work alongside their foreign colleagues.
- Whatever your personal professional development needs, there is now the opportunity to refresh your language and pedagogical skills. CILT Regional Support Groups now offer free twilight ELL methodology sessions to primary teachers who wish to set up schemes in their own school (see Chapter 5).

WHAT DO I NEED TO KNOW?

After piloting their Modern Languages in the Primary School project (MLPS) from 1989–1994 the Scots drew up a useful list of 'competences' to define the essential skills and knowledge required of a primary languages teacher, as follows.

A knowledge of:

- *the sound system of the language – accurate pronunciation/intonation;*
- *the alphabet and numbers;*
- *personal language – talking about yourself, your family, your home;*
- *descriptive language – people, animals, clothes, houses, etc;*
- *affective language – likes/dislikes, feelings, emotions, aches and pains, praise, etc;*
- *language needed for classroom organisation, for praise and rewards;*
- *language needed to deal with other areas of the curriculum – Maths, Art, Craft, ICT, Science, etc;*
- *language needed for playing games, reciting poems, singing songs, storytelling, acting and mime.*

Modern Languages in the primary school – competences (Johnstone 1994a)

This range of linguistic knowledge cannot be built up overnight without expert training, but most of what is outlined in the above list is available in print or on video to teachers who do not have access to local INSET (see 'Where can I get help?', p56).

In a nutshell, you will initially need only a small repertoire of classroom phrases to start and finish the lesson and to organise activities in the course of the lesson; and the usual daily routines: register, lunches, this is what we are going to do today …

And of course you will need to do your homework on the language specific to whichever topic you are dealing with this week: birthdays, school, pets, leisure activities, etc …

Whichever year group you are teaching, we would recommend scripting for yourself a handful of phrases you intend to use each week (as in the table below) and sticking them to your desk as a constant reminder. Once your class has heard them often enough and shown that they understand them, you should make sure you keep on using the same key greetings, instructions and questions over a period of weeks until you are sure that all the children understand them and respond appropriately. Then you can gradually add a new 'phrase of the week' to expand their repertoire (see 'Planning for progression', p19).

Sample phrases/instructions

Bonjour! Ça va?
Alex, tais-toi!
Tracey, assieds-toi!
Ecoutez!
Aujourd'hui, on va … chanter.
　　　　　　　　écouter la cassette.
　　　　　　　　regarder une video.
　　　　　　　　compter de 0 à 10.
Bon! Silence, s'il vous plaît!
Taisez-vous!
Rangez vos affaires!
Au revoir! A demain! A vendredi!

F

Guten Tag! Wie geht's?
Alex, sei still!
Tracey, setz dich!
Hört zu!
Heute wollen wir ... singen.
　　　　　　　uns die Kassette anhören.
　　　　　　　uns ein Video anschauen.
　　　　　　　von Null bis 10 zählen.
Also gut! Ruhe, bitte!
Seid bitte ruhig!
Räumt eure Sachen zusammen!
Auf Wiedersehen! Bis morgen! Bis Freitag!

¡Buenos días! ¡Qué tal?
¡Alex, silencio por favor!
¡Tracey, siéntate!
¡Escuchadme bien!
Hoy vamos a ... cantar.
　　　　　　　escuchar una cinta.
　　　　　　　ver un video.
　　　　　　　contar de 0 a 10.
¡Silencio!
¡Silencio por favor!
¡Guardad vuestras cosas!
¡Adiós a todos! ¡Hasta mañana! ¡Hasta el viernes!

NB These instructions should always be accompanied by the appropriate gesture to reinforce meaning.

If you begin with a relatively small and easily memorable set of short, simple phrases – accompanied of course by lots of mime and body language! – the class will understand easily and begin to respond. As Jayne Patten, Advisory Teacher for Liverpool LEA, points out: 'This vital first time a learner encounters the new language must be **memorable** in order for the language to stick! The learners need to hear and repeat the language many times if they are to internalise it and produce it independently.' So do not hesitate to use lots of colourful visuals, amusing gestures and emphasis on unusual sounds.

As your confidence grows and pupils' comprehension improves you will find it is possible to conduct more and more of the lesson in the target language without having to use English (but see p57 'How much target language? How much English?').

In time you will be able to add more variations to the basic phrases you began with, as we have illustrated in Chapter 2, and expose your children to gradually more demanding sentences and texts. Ultimately you should aim to give virtually all your classroom instructions in the target language, reserving English for explaining the more complex concepts of grammar, cultural differences in the foreign country, or the rules of a new game.

To help you make a start we have reproduced in the Appendix a very basic list of classroom language (teacher language) in French, German, Spanish. This should see you through most of your first year, but will need to be added to as you make progress.

WHAT DO THE CHILDREN NEED TO KNOW?

Having chosen your own small stock of management phrases, you will need to plan a small package of key phrases, mostly questions, that the children will need to learn in order to communicate their needs and feelings to you: a sort of 'survival kit' that discourages them from resorting to English every time they want to ask you something. You will find a fuller discussion of this in Young Pathfinder 4: *Keep talking* (Satchwell 1997), Chapter 1, but here are the sort of phrases they will need:

Asking for ...

help

Répétez, s'il vous plaît!	*Noch einmal, bitte!*	*¡Repetid por favor!*
Madame, je ne comprends pas (je n'ai pas compris).	*Ich verstehe nicht (ich habe nicht verstanden).*	*Señora, no entiendo, no comprendo.*
Vous pouvez m'aider, s'il vous plaît?	*Können Sie mir helfen, bitte?*	*¿Puede ayudarme por favor?*

explanation

Comment dit-on en français ... XYZ?	*Wie sagt man auf Deutsch ... XYZ?*	*¿Cómo se dice en español ... XYZ?*
C'est quoi en anglais?	*Wie heißt das auf Englisch?*	*¿Cómo se dice en inglés?*

equipment

Je n'ai pas de ... crayons de couleurs.	*Ich habe keine ... Farbstifte.*	*No tengo ... lapices de colores.*

where something is

Où sont les ciseaux, s'il vous plaît?	*Wo ist die Schere, bitte?*	*¿Dónde estan las tijeras?*

permission

Je peux aller aux toilettes, s'il vous plaît?	*Darf ich auf die Toilette gehen, bitte?*	*¿Puedo ir al servicio?*
On peut baisser les stores, s'il vous plaît?	*Dürfen wir die Jalousien herunterlassen, bitte?*	*¿Puedo abrir la persiana?*

and making apologies and excuses

Excusez-moi, Madame. J'ai oublié mon sac à dos.	*Entschuldigen Sie, Frau A. Ich habe meine Schultasche vergessen.*	*Disculpe señora, me he olvidado la bolsa.*

It is very helpful to the children if you display such phrases (with visuals!) on a frieze round the classroom walls or as mobiles from the ceiling.

The children will also need to learn a few phrases for playing card and board games, occasional playground games (e.g. 'Hopscotch') and for carrying out role-play tasks. These are all elaborated further in Young Pathfinder 4: *Keep talking* (Satchwell 1997), Chapter 1; in Young Pathfinder 2: *Games and fun activities* (Martin 1995), Chapters 3 and 4; and in the greatest detail in *Ici on parle français, Wir sprechen Deutsch* and *Se habla Español* (McColl et al 1997, 1999 and 2000).

 ## WHAT SORTS OF LANGUAGE?

The language of classroom interaction can be split into three basic categories.

Most of the first type of interaction (**Teacher–pupil**) will consist of instructions and questions, but we hope there will be comments, praise and expressions of surprise – as well as the occasional reprimands!

Most of the second type (**Pupil–teacher**) will be the survival-kit language we have already referred to, but as children progress they will want to express more complex ideas and feelings and try to say what **they** want to say, even if in rather hesitant and faulty French, German, Spanish – a kind of meta-language which we should expect and encourage! We do, after all, want the children to be adventurous and experiment with the new language; so they should be encouraged to be creative in forming sentences and dialogues of their own.

Pupil–pupil language is essential for the children if they are going to play games and act out scenes, stories and role play.

These aspects of classroom communication are discussed fully in Young Pathfinder 4: *Keep talking* (Satchwell 1997), Chapter 1; in Young Pathfinder 2: *Games and fun activities* (Martin 1995); and in Young Pathfinder 6: *Let's join in!* (Martin and Cheater 1998).

WHERE CAN I GET HELP?

Numerous sources of help are now available to enable you to expand and consolidate your stock of target-language phrases. Obviously, if you can find a native speaker to act as your personal 'linguistic consultant' you may be able to use him or her as a walking dictionary. A few enlightened LEAs have recently appointed Foreign Language Assistants to work exclusively in a group of primary schools and these young people are a godsend to language teachers in providing a model of pronunciation and intonation, up-to-date language and a source of variations on the phrases they already know.

Some LEAs host trainee teachers from abroad who come to the UK for a few weeks as part of their initial teacher training. The exciting and rewarding possibilities of working with a native speaker in your classroom are explored in detail in Young Pathfinder 12: *Working together* (Martin and Farren 2004).

Failing access to any of these, you can consult any of the following resources to help you expand your target language.

The **videos** of classroom materials produced by KETV and by Early Start Languages:

- French: *Pilote 1, 2* and *3* (KETV)
             Early Start French 1 and *2* (Early Start Languages)
             Pilote interactive CD-ROM 2: *'Mon école'* (KETV)
- German: *3, 2, 1... los!* (KETV)
- Spanish: *Early Start Spanish: Tú y yo* and *Mi ciudad y mi colegio* (Early Start Languages)

All of these packs provide excellent, user-friendly teacher's notes and a good basic stock of classroom language which will help even the least confident teacher to get started.

The **course materials** produced by ELI for primary French:

• *Avant Gaston, Gaston 1* and *2*, and more recently *Hélico 1*, *2* and *3* have clear teacher's guides (all in simple French!) and good audiocassettes.

So also have the three parts of *Ja klar!* which offers equally helpful material in German. You will find here simple phrases and instructions relating to all the common topic areas we outlined in Chapter 1.

ELI also publishes excellent **pupil workbooks** full of fun activities, for revision and consolidation to go with *Hélico* and *Ja klar!*

The *Lehrerhandbuch* to *Tamburin 1* and *2* (clearly laid out in simple German) is also helpful for target language and full of excellent ideas for classroom activities (Hueber/European Schoolbooks).

For veritable 'bibles' containing teacher and pupil target language as well as many ideas for learning games there are nothing more comprehensive than *Ici on parle français, Wir sprechen Deutsch* and *Se habla español* (MLG Publishing). These are real mines of information. Each of these books contains pages of games and activities based round photocopiable cartoon pictures covering all the classroom situations and topics you are ever likely to need in primary school. They also provide a comprehensive dictionary of classroom target-language phrases listed by topic/situation and recorded on audiocassette.

To see examples of UK primary teachers using the target language in a variety of ways with children from Reception classes to Year 6, working in French, German and Spanish we would recommend the CILT Early Language Learning videos (2001–2003), *Making it happen, Making it work* and *Making it better.* These will provide you with ideas about valid approaches and early language-learning methodology as well as encouragement to try the activities in your own classroom.

You will find-down-to earth help with classroom language, instructions for games, songs and rhymes in Young Pathfinder 2: *Games and fun activities* (Martin 1995) and Young Pathfinder 6: *Let's join in!* (Martin and Cheater 1998).

The CILT ResourceFile 2: *Up, up and away!* (Elston 2000) has some excellent ideas for providing the children with 'survival-kit' language – as well as ready-made classroom posters plus visuals with practical tips on how to make your own.

HOW MUCH TARGET LANGUAGE? HOW MUCH ENGLISH?

As we said at the beginning, you should endeavour to expose your class to as much target language as possible during the week. But it is important not to alienate the children by speaking **only** in the foreign language in the first few weeks. With KS1 children their concentration span is short and a constant change of activities is essential. There must be deliberate 'breathers' – parts of the lesson when the children know they will be able to ask you for explanations in

English of things they did not understand, meanings of individual words, and a slot for explanations of some of the more tricky aspects of foreign culture that you could not get across to them in the target language. How long the English slots should be, only you can decide, but it is important to make clear to the children what the rules are and when you are going to change from one language to the other. One teacher we know has two boards in her class, one entitled 'Deutsch' and the other 'English'. The children know immediately which language to speak, as English is allowed only when she points to that board!

Remember, a French lesson is not a French lesson when 90% of it is conducted in English, nor when the teacher gives an immediate translation of what he or she has just said! If you realise that some of your slower pupils have got left behind, why not use one of your brighter pupils as the 'interpreter' rather than doing it yourself? By the end of the first year you should be aiming at around 80% in the target language for most lessons.

EXPOSING CHILDREN TO THE TARGET LANGUAGE

The class teacher has far more opportunity than his or her secondary colleagues or peripatetic colleagues to immerse the children in the target language. Not only does he or she have the scope to display key phrases around the room (friezes, charts, mobiles; see ResourceFile 2: *Up, up and away!* (Elston 2000)), to set up a foreign language shop or realia corner in the classroom, but can use odd moments in the day to fit in a quick recap of a song, a rhyme, a tongue-twister or of phrases they learned yesterday! And with some enterprise and negotiation he or she can extend the display around the school corridors so that visitors are welcomed in two or more languages, and photographs and posters show which languages are spoken in your school.

Even more impact is made on the children if a Foreign Language Assistant is shared with other primary schools in the area. His or her presence once or twice a week really brings the new language to life for your pupils and encourages them to try it out for real. A Foreign Language Assistant can also make a major cultural impact on the rest of your staff, including the headteacher!

Similarly, a link with a primary school abroad will bring huge benefits and motivation in the form of exchange of pupils' work, photographs, videos, work on common projects (e.g. a Comenius project), e-pals, etc – bringing an international dimension into the whole school. You can find out how to link your school with a partner school abroad by consulting the British Council Global Gateway website (**www.globalgateway.org.uk**).

Parents can also provide invaluable support to the classroom teacher if they are willing to reinforce your all too brief language lessons by following up at home. The CILT book *Bringing it home* (Farren and Smith 2003) has many suggestions to show how parents can reinforce the foreign language lessons in school by using simple rhymes, songs and games at home.

HOW SHOULD I PLAN THE TARGET LANGUAGE?

Even with a relatively modest command of the language you can sustain lessons in the target language if you plan your lessons carefully and script the phrases you intend to use. We have suggested below a possible model for doing this in French. See also the basic lists of classroom language (in French, German and Spanish) in the Appendix.

But you must keep the target language very simple, both for yourself and the children. Short snappy phrases, even one-word instructions (with gestures!), are more readily understood and memorised. Long sentences merely go over the heads of pupils and confuse them.

Complicated explanations – of some cultural aspect, e.g. the difference between *tu* and *vous, du* and *Sie, tú* and *Usted*, or an explanation of mealtimes in France or the schoolday in Spain, and of course any critical grammar point – are all best dealt with in English.

EXAMPLES

---

1. TALKING ABOUT YOUR SCHOOL BAG AND ITS CONTENTS (KS1)

Teacher	Pupil
Où est ton sac à dos?	*Mon sac à dos? Voilà!*
Voila! Merci. Et toi, où est ton sac?	*Voilà!*
Et qu'est-ce qu'il y a dans ton sac à dos?	*(Dans mon sac) il y a …*
	un/une … deux/trois …
Montre-moi!	
Est-ce qu'il y a un/une … crayon/gomme/stylo?	*Oui … voilà … une gomme.*
	Non, il n'y pas de … crayons.
De quelle couleur est … ton stylo/ta trousse?	*Rouge/blanc/gris …*
Est-ce qu'il y a un stylo noir/vert/rouge?	*Oui … il y a un stylo rouge.*
Est-ce que tu as …?	*J'ai un/une …*

Game:

> *Montre-moi/donne-moi un/une … gomme/*
> *règle/taille-crayons. Voilà!*

---

2. TALKING ABOUT BIRTHDAYS (KS2)

Teacher	Pupil
Moi, j'ai quarante ans.	
Et toi, Lucy? Quel âge as-tu?	*J'ai 7 ans.*
Mon anniversaire, c'est en mai.	
C'est quand ton anniversaire?	*En juin.*
Et toi? Quelle est la date de ton anniversaire?	*C'est le cinq janvier.*
Qui a son anniversaire en janvier/février?	*Moi! En février.*
Lève-toi, si ton anniversaire est en juillet/ en avril …	actions
Et aujourd'hui, c'est l'anniversaire de Brian.	
Bon anniversaire, Brian!	
Vas-y! Souffle les bougies!	*(Il souffle les bougies.)*

Song: *Bon anniversaire!*

5. Support and resources

 ## INITIAL TEACHER TRAINING

As we noted in the introduction, since 2001 there has been a steady expansion of Primary PGCE courses now offering a foreign language element. The Teacher Training Agency (TTA) and CILT worked initially with just five higher education (HE) colleges, making links with training institutions in France to set up reciprocal visits to primary schools as part of the programme. The handful of PGCE students in 2001 has recently expanded and the reciprocal training programmes now include Spain, Germany, Italy and Portugal. There is patently no shortage of applicants wishing to teach a language in primary school!

We are fully aware that the Primary PGCE course in any HE college still means squeezing a 'quart into a pint pot'; there is so much to do in nine months and never enough time to go into any aspect of the curriculum in great enough depth. It is encouraging therefore that the TTA is beginning to restore some of the three- or four-year B Ed and BA/QTS courses with a foreign language strand which had almost ceased to exist between 1990 and 2000. This should enable colleges to provide a thorough language development course – to take students from GCSE level to A level equivalent in their chosen language – combined with ELL methodology; and the course can now include more in-depth studies of the language and culture of the foreign country, with a study period/teaching practice abroad, building on the pattern of reciprocal arrangements already in place.

 ## CONTINUING PROFESSIONAL DEVELOPMENT

Ten years ago there was little in-service support for teachers of languages in primary schools outside the handful of LEAs such as Kent, Surrey, and Richmond upon Thames, which had Advisory Teachers and in-service training programmes to support teachers in the classroom. Now there is much wider coverage and ever-increasing interest in sharing good practice: nineteen ELL 'Pathfinder' LEAs have recently received Government funding for the expansion of primary languages provision, and LEAs such as Liverpool, East Riding, Sheffield, and South Gloucestershire have made their own major local commitments in terms of funding, Advisory Teachers, Foreign Language Assistants and continuing professional development programmes.

On top of these local initiatives there are the nationally organised courses, conferences and languages shows run by CILT. INSET opportunities in the regions have been greatly enhanced by the creation of CILT Regional Support Groups for Early Language Learning – and some of the HE colleges are now providing similar services in their own areas. These are all listed on the NACELL website.

Nevertheless, these arrangements still do not provide blanket coverage for primary schools in all parts of England. There are still blank areas with no Languages Adviser, no Advisory Teachers and no expertise in ELL provision. If you are teaching in one of the latter, we suggest you take up the issue with your LEA, requesting support, and make contact with your nearest ELL Regional Support Group or Comenius Centre for help and advice.

We have listed below as many support mechanisms as we are aware of in early 2004.

 ## CPD OPPORTUNITIES FOR PRIMARY TEACHERS

NATIONAL

The central base for information on early language learning in the UK is the NACELL Library for ELL resources at CILT. Teachers can access the full range of literature, view videos and other resources here.

If London is beyond your reach you will find plenty of information on the NACELL website: **www.nacell.org.uk**. Here you will find examples of good practice and schemes of work in the *NACELL best practice guide* and descriptions of a large range of useful classroom resources.

CILT residential courses for primary teachers held in France, Spain, Germany, Italy: **www.cilt. org.uk/cpd/index.htm**.

CILT Conferences: Primary Languages Show (two days) held every spring.

CILT CPD courses for primary teachers: one-day and five-session courses over two terms.

ALL Language World conference: three-day conference for language teachers in all sectors held every spring.

REGIONAL

Comenius Centres (see **www.cilt.org.uk/comenius/index.htm**)

CILT ELL Regional Support Groups – five free twilight sessions per year (**www.nacell.org.uk/ regional/index.htm**).

LEAs
Nineteen 'Pathfinder' LEAs received Government funding to support and develop ELL provision in their primary schools. Other LEAs may have set up their own primary languages initiatives. It is worth enquiring of your own LEA what is planned between now and 2010!

Higher education colleges
Some HE colleges have set up ELL support courses for primary teachers in their area (e.g. York, Lancaster, Southampton) and we hope that more will follow.

PUBLISHED RESOURCES AND CLASSROOM MATERIALS

The volume and scope of teaching resources available to primary languages teachers has expanded enormously in recent years. While primary Italian is still not well served, teachers of French, German and Spanish and now have a whole gamut of resources – books, workbooks, worksheets, games and puzzles, audio- and videocassettes, CDs, CD-ROMs and websites at their disposal.

The following resources list is as comprehensive as we can manage in this small book, but it is by no means exhaustive. We have listed resources in French, German and Spanish that we have used ourselves, reviewed or had recommended to us.

You will find many more materials listed on the NACELL website, in the CILT Information Sheets and in the European Schoolbooks catalogue: 'Languages for younger learners'.

Fortunately, publishers all over Europe are now producing ELL materials on a regular basis. You can be sure there are still more in the pipeline!

Whatever resources you eventually choose to use in your own classroom, we would urge you to do some thorough research and evaluation of the materials before ordering for your school. Funds are so scarce that you cannot afford to make a mistake on a major investment. Make sure that the materials match the age and maturity of your class; that they cover the topics and the language structures set out in your scheme of work – and that the tasks and activities are the kind you are happy to work with.

It is particularly important to vet computer software and, if at all possible, to work through it yourself before purchasing it. If you can, make a half-day visit to the NACELL Library at CILT to browse through the full range of materials in all media. If that is not feasible, you will find a great deal of help on the NACELL website which has a special resources section with a brief decription of most of the latest published materials.

If you feel your pupils are ready to use Internet sites (full of authentic language!), we would strongly recommend you to try out those in Dan Tierney's list first (p71); you can easily waste many precious hours browsing sites that turn out to be useless or quite inappropriate for your classes!

CILT INFORMATION SHEETS

52 *Teaching materials for young beginners: French*
53 *Teaching materials for young beginners: German*
54 *ICT teaching materials for early language learning*
55 *Languages for young beginners: reports and guides*
93 *Teaching materials for young beginners: Italian*
94 *Teaching materials for young beginners: Spanish*

All of these free information sheets are updated annually.

PROFESSIONAL BACKGROUND READING FOR TEACHERS

WEBSITES

INFORMATION

National Advisory Centre on Early Language Learning (NACELL): **www.nacell.org.uk**
Early Language Learning discussion forum: **www.nacell.org.uk/networking/ ell_forum.htm**
QCA, Scheme of Work for KS2: **www.standards.dfes.gov.uk/schemes/primary_mfl/ ?view=get**
The British Council website offers help to teachers in making contact with schools abroad: **www.britishcouncil.org/education**

BOOK SUPPLIERS/PUBLISHERS

Amazon Germany: **www.amazon.de**
Amazon France: **www.amazon.fr**
Fnac (French bookseller): **www.fnac.com**
Nathan (French publisher): **www.nathan.fr**
Young Europeans Bookstore: **www.youngLinguists.com**

TEACHING RESOURCES

BBC Primary French: **www.bbc.co.uk/schools/primaryfrench**
BBC Primary Spanish: **www.bbc.co.uk/schools/primaryspanish**
Channel 4: **www.channel4.com/modernlanguages; www.channel4.com/primary**
Kindernetz: **www.kindernetz.de**
Momes.net: **www.momes.net**

VIDEOS DEALING WITH ORGANISATION, TEACHING APPROACHES AND ELL METHODOLOGY

An early start: German in the primary school. Goethe-Institut.
European awareness in primary schools. Central Bureau/British Council.

EARLY LANGUAGE LEARNING VIDEOS, CILT

ELL video 1: *Making it happen: How teachers plan for linguistic progression.*
ELL video 2: *Making it work: How teachers plan, motivate – and integrate.*
ELL video 3: *Making it better: How primary pupils are getting off to a flying start in learning a foreign language.*

These three videos provide an excellent introduction to ELL and give an insight into the variety of approaches that have been adopted in the UK. The principles of good practice are discussed in some detail and primary teachers from all over England have been filmed with their classes from Reception to Year 6. There are clips from French, German and Spanish lessons.

VIDEO TRAINING MATERIALS FOR THE TEACHER

Travail d'instit. Didier/European Schoolbooks. (Useful for target language in classroom management; native speakers in French primary schools)
Une vie d'instit. Didier/European Schoolbooks. (French primary teachers describe their work and schools)
Lehrer erzählen. Didier/European Schoolbooks. (German primary teachers describe their work and schools)

BOOKS ON METHODOLOGY/PEDAGOGY

Huge strides have been made in the field of ELL in the last five years and the books/journal listed below provide a detailed look at primary pedagogy and organisational issues:

Teaching Modern Languages at primary school (Johnstone). SCRE.
The teaching of Modern Foreign Languages in the primary school (ed. Driscoll and Frost). Routledge.
Modern Foreign Languages in the primary school – the what, why and how of early language teaching (Sharpe). Kogan Page.
Young learners (Phillips). Oxford University Press. (Contains a wealth of ideas for classroom activities in primary languages classes)
Journal: Frühes Deutsch (formerly *PRIMAR*). Goethe-Institut/Bertelsmann. (In German; appears three times a year. More than thirty issues so far covering all aspects of teaching German as a foreign language in primary schools across the world)

The books listed below focus on the practical aspects of classroom methodology and have been written as short teachers' guides:

CILT *YOUNG PATHFINDER* SERIES

Young Pathfinder 2:	*Games and fun activities* (Martin)
Young Pathfinder 3:	*Are you sitting comfortably? Telling stories to young learners* (Tierney and Dobson)
Young Pathfinder 4:	*Keep talking! Teaching in the target language* (Satchwell)
Young Pathfinder 5:	*First steps to reading and writing* (Skarbek)
Young Pathfinder 6:	*Let's join in! Rhymes, poems, songs* (Martin and Cheater)
Young Pathfinder 7:	*Making the link: Relating languages to other work in the school* (Tierney and Hope)
Young Pathfinder 8:	*Grammar is fun!* (Biriotti)
Young Pathfinder 9:	*The literacy link* (Cheater and Farren)
Young Pathfinder 10:	*A world of languages! Developing children's love of languages* (Datta and Pomphrey)
Young Pathfinder 12:	*Working together: Native speakers in the primary school* (Martin and Farren)

also *Bringing it home: How parents can support children's language learning* (Farren and Smith)

ResourceFile 2: *Up, up and away! Using classroom target language to help learners say what they want to say* (Elston)

ResourceFile 3: *Getting the basics right: Nouns, gender and adjectives* (Biriotti)

ResourceFile 5: *A modern image: Enhancing the use of the OHP* (Tierney and Humphreys)

ResourceFile 6: *Rhythm and rhyme: Developing language in French and German* (Martin)

 ## PRIMARY CLASSROOM 'COURSE' MATERIALS WITH HELPFUL TEACHER'S GUIDES

French
Avant Gaston. ELI/European Schoolbooks.
C'est français. Brilliant Publications.
Collins Primary French Starter Pack. Collins.
Comète 1 and *2.* Oxford University Press.
Entre dans la Ronde. La Jolie Ronde Ltd.
Gaston 1, 2 and 3. ELI/European Schoolbooks.
Hélico 1, 2 and 3. ELI/European Schoolbooks.
Hélico au pays des jouets. ELI/European Schoolbooks.
Hélico en vacances 1, 2 and *3.* ELI/European Schoolbooks.
Le petit trampoline. CLE/European Schoolbooks.
La ronde des petits. La Jolie Ronde Ltd.

German
Hallo, da bin ich! Cornelsen/European Schoolbooks.
Ja klar! 1, 2 and *3.* ELI/European Schoolbooks.
Tamburin 1 and *2.* Hueber/European Schoolbooks.
Wer? Wie? Was? Mega 1 and *2.* GILDE/European Schoolbooks.

Spanish
!Bienvenidos! 1, 2 and *3.* ELI/European Schoolbooks.
Me gusta: Español oral en primaria. Spanish Embassy.
Pasacalle 1 and *2.* SGEL/European Schoolbooks.
Una Rayuela 1. SGEL/European Schoolbooks.
Los trotamundos 1 and *2.* Edelsa/European Schoolbooks.

 ## VIDEO CLASSROOM MATERIALS WITH HELPFUL TEACHER'S GUIDES

French
Chez Mimi. 4-Learning.
Le club. BBC.
Early Start French 1 and *2.* Early Start Languages.
Hocus & Lotus. CILT.

Pilote 1, 2 and *3*. KETV.
Salut Serge! BBC.

German
3, 2, 1 … los! KETV.
Hennings Haus. 4-Learning.
Hocus & Lotus. CILT.

Spanish
Hocus & Lotus. CILT.
Mi ciudad y mi colegio. Early Start Languages.
La tienda de Luis. 4-Learning.
Tu y yo! Early Start Languages.

 ## CD-ROMs

Bambolo. Julia Emily Software. (Years 2–4. French, Italian)
Le corbeau et la sorcière. Hatier.
Le goûter de Margot. Hatier.
Hexaglot glotto. Hexaglot Software. (Years 2–4. French, German, Italian, Spanish)
Le jour de Charlotte. Hatier.
Lecture primaire. Revilo. (Reading practice for beginners)
Le mystère des lizards. Hatier.
Pilote interactive 1 and *2*. KETV. (Interactive French course for young beginners)
Les surprises de Boub. Hatier. (KS2)
Lektüre Grundstufe. Revilo.
Mein erstes Lexikon. Duden/Dorling Kindersley. (KS2)

 ### Games and classroom activities (mostly with photocopiable worksheets)

French
Carte blanche primaire. Revilo.
Chante Noël! Merryman Primary Resources.
Fêtes et festivals. Merryman Primary Resources.
Ici on parle français. MLG Publishing.
Jeux faciles. LCP.
Joyeux Noël! LJR.
The LCP Language Games Pack. LCP. (Contains over 60 games + photocopiable sheets)
Ouvre la porte! Merryman Primary Resources.
Quatre saisons: Action verse/songs. Merryman Primary Resources.

German

Superspiele. LCP.
Wer? Wie? Was? Schatzkiste. GILDE/European Schoolbooks.
Wir sprechen Deutsch. MLG Publishing.

Spanish

Juegos fáciles. LCP.
Se habla español. MLG Publishing.

VISUAL AIDS/FLASHCARDS, ETC ALL IN FRENCH, GERMAN AND SPANISH

Active posters. ELI/European Schoolbooks.
240 flashcards for primary school beginners. ELI/European Schoolbooks.
ELI class clock. European Schoolbooks.
Elikits. ELI/European Schoolbooks. (Boxed sets of audiovisual tools: flashcards, bingo cards, counters, teacher's guide; five kits covering: animals, house, clothes, food, actions)
Masks set. ELI/European Schoolbooks. (16 humorous masks for role play)

LISTENING MATERIALS

!Escuchame! (Bevis). LCP.
Hörquiz (Bevis). LCP.
Quiz-écoutes (Bevis). LCP.

SONGBOOKS

French

Le français en chantant. Didier/European Schoolbooks. (Activity book and cassette)
Usborne French Songbook. Usborne.

German

Detlev Jöcker: Seine schönsten Lieder. Menschenkinder Verlag.
Die schönsten Kinderlieder und Kinderreime. Bassermann.
Die schönsten Kinderlieder zum singen und musizieren. Nikol.

Spanish

Mi libro de canciones. Fun Languages.

SONGS AND RAPS ON CDS/AUDIO-CASSETTES

French

1, 2, 3 soleil! Husar/European Schoolbooks. (Book: 66 songs; cassette: 30 songs)
1, 2, 3 techno. Husar/European Schoolbooks. (Book: 66 songs; cassette: 30 songs)

101 poésies et comptines. Bayard.
ABC pour commencer. CIDEB/European Schoolbooks.
Les chansons et les raps de Monsieur X. David Hicks (Contact: david.hicks@ntlworld.com)
Chantons tous! LCP.
Français! Français! LCP.
Henri Dès. (Numerous song collections, see **www.henrides.com**)
Petites chansons pour tous les jours. Nathan.
Poésies, comptines et chansons pour Noël. Gallimard Jeunesse. (Cassette or CD)
Sing and learn French. European Schoolbooks.
Sing your way to French. European Schoolbooks.

Spanish
1, 2, 3 salsa!. Husar/European Schoolbooks. (Book: 66 songs; cassette: 30 songs)
Sing and learn Spanish. European Schoolbooks. (Book plus CD)

German
Detlev Jöcker. Menschenkinder Verlag.
* *1, 2, 3 im Sauseschritt*
* *Ich bin der kleine Zappelmann*
* *Mile male mule, ich gehe in die Schule*
* *Und weiter geht's im Sauseschritt*

Start German with a song (Jöcker/Fuhrig). Menschenkinder Verlag/Goethe-Institut. (12 songs + Teacher's notes)

 ## SONGS ON VIDEO

French
Au claire de la lune. Folimage.
Chansons Henri Dès en images. Folimage. (13 songs)
Le karaoke de Noël. ELI/European Schoolbooks.
Mon âne 1 and *2.* Folimage.
Mr Ficelle – fun French. Pop English Creations. European Schoolbooks.
Voilà le karaoke. ELI/European schoolbooks.

German
Das Weihnachtskaraoke. ELI/European Schoolbooks.

Spanish
El karaoke de los trotamundos. Edelsa/European Schoolbooks.

 ## REWARDS AND STICKERS

See **www.nacell.org.uk/resources/resources.htm** for details of companies offering foreign language stickers.

DICTIONARIES

DICTIONARIES FOR THE TEACHER'S DESK

Collins first time French dictionary. Harper Collins.
New Pocket French/German/Italian/Spanish Dictionary in colour. Collins Education.

PICTURE/FIRST DICTIONARIES

Der ABC-Duden. European Schoolbooks.
Easy learning French/German/Italian/Spanish Dictionaries. Collins.
ELI picture dictionary. European Schoolbooks. (KS2; French, German, Italian, Spanish)
ELI picture dictionary junior. ELI/European Schoolbooks. (French, German, Italian, Spanish)
First 100 words in French. Usborne.
First time French dictionary. KS2. Collins.
First time French dictionary skills. Collins. (KS2; photocopiable worksheets + ideas for teachers)
French/German/Italian/Spanish Dictionary for Beginners. Usborne.
Mein erstes deutsches Bildwörterbuch. ELI/European Schoolbooks.
Mi primer diccionario ilustrado de español. ELI/European Schoolbooks.
Mon premier dictionnaire illustré de français. ELI/European Schoolbooks.
Usborne book of everyday words. Usborne. (Sticker book: French/German/Italian/Spanish)

BIG BOOKS

Raconte et chante series. ELI/European Schoolbooks:
• *A la mer*
• *Anniversaire à la ferme*
• *Les amis de la ferme*
• *Monsieur l'arbre et la petite fille*
• *Plic ... plic tombe la pluie*
• *Un pique-nique*

READING MATERIALS/SIMPLE READERS

French
Album des monstres. LCP. (10 short readers)
Galaxie 1, 2, 3. Heinemann. (Rigby Star readers in French)
Lecture primaire – CD-ROM. Revilo.
Les petits Lascars – Je lis et j'écris 1, 2, 3. Didier/European Schoolbooks.
Magazines: *Allons-y!*, etc. Mary Glasgow Magazines.
Magazines: *Voilà; Fertig ... los!; !Vamos!.* ELI/European Schoolbooks.
Plaisir de lire – série verte. ELI/European Schoolbooks.

German

Lesen leicht gemacht – die grüne Reihe. ELI/European Schoolbooks. (Collection of well-known fairy tales and *Märchen*, with cassettes)
Lesen leicht gemacht – fabelhafte Fabeln. ELI/European Schoolbooks. (Collection of simple readers adapted from fables, with cassettes) ELI/European Schoolbooks

Spanish

Mis primeras cuentas – Las fabulas fabulosas. ELI/European Schoolbooks. (Collection of simple readers adapted from fables, with cassettes)
Mis primeras cuentas – Serie verde. ELI/European Schoolbooks. (Collection of simple readers adapted from well-known fairy tales, with cassettes)

TOURING THEATRE AND DRAMA GROUPS

European Theatre Company: **www.europeantheatre.co.uk**
Théâtre sans frontières: **www.theatresansfrontieres.co.uk**
Whisper and Shout: perform in French/German/Italian. Tel: 01452 419 039

FOREIGN LANGUAGE WEBSITES SUITABLE FOR PRIMARY CHILDREN

We would strongly recommend teachers to read the very helpful advice in Young Pathfinder 9: *The literacy link* (Cheater and Farren 2001) on 'Using the Internet to develop reading and writing skills'(p67). You will need to ask yourself, for example:

- How appropriate is the subject and the language content?
- What adaptation will be required?
- What prior knowledge will the pupils need?
- What new knowledge will the pupils gain?
- What follow-up activities will be possible?

With all websites and CD-ROMs, we would strongly recommend teachers to work through them carefully themselves to see whether the material is really at an appropriate level for their pupils.

We are indebted to Dan Tierney (University of Strathclyde) for the following list of websites containing material suitable for primary school pupils. The list was compiled in early 2004, but teachers need to be aware that websites come and go with amazing rapidity, so be prepared for deletions or replacements every few months.

	French	German	Spanish
Gateways	www.yahoo.fr www.ecole-plus.com www. sitespourenfants.com	www.lycos.de	www.yahoo.es
Colours	http://fr.coloriage.com	http://de.coloriage.com	http://es.coloriage.com
Festivals	www.vivelesfetes.net	http://navidaddigital.com	
Games	http://uptoten.com http:// auxpetitesmains. free.fr www.quia.com www. pouletfrites.com www.chez-merlin.com www.spellmaster.com	http://blinde-kuh.de http://kidsweb.de www. kindernetz.de http:// kidsville.de	www.donquijote.org
Penpals www. wotw.org.uk	www.momes.net	www.schulweb.de	www.chicos.net.ar
Self/greetings	www.fr.greetings. yahoo.com http:// fr.uptoten.com www. teteamodeler.com	http://de.greetings. yahoo.com http:// grusskarten.de	http://es.greetings. yahoo.com
Shopping	www.carrefour.com	www.coop.ch	www.elcorteingles.es
Songs	http://auxpetitesmains. free.fr http://henrides.com	http://detlevjoecker.de	
Travel/railway timetables www. easyjet.com (in 4 languages)	www.sncf.com http:// opodo.fr	www.bahn.de	www.renfe.es

USEFUL ADDRESSES

Comenius Centres: **www.cilt.org.uk/comenius/index.htm**
Regional Support Groups for Early Language Learning: **www.nacell.org.uk/regional/index.htm**

PUBLISHERS

See **www.nacell.org.uk** for details.

Appendix: Classroom language – a basic starting list

We have provided here as a *point de départ* a very short basic list in French, German and Spanish.

Classroom language	Ce qu'on dit en classe	Was sagt man in der Klasse?	¿Lo que se dice en clase?
Greetings	**Pour saluer**	**Grüssen**	**Saludes**
Hello	Bonjour!	Guten Morgen!	¡Buenos días!
Hello, children	Bonjour les enfants!	Guten Morgen, Kinder!	¡Buenos días niños!/a todos!
	Salut!	Guten Tag! Grüß Gott!	
Are you OK?	Ça va?	Wie geht's?	¿Que tal?
How are you?	Comment vas-tu?	Wie geht's dir?	¿Y tù?
I'm very well, thank you	Je vais bien, très bien, merci	Danke, gut Sehr gut, danke	Estoy muy bien, gracias
I'm not well	Je ne vais pas bien	Nicht gut	Estoy mal
What's wrong with you?	Qu'est-ce que tu as?	Nun, was hast du denn?	¿Porqé estás mal?
Starting the lesson	**Pour commencer**	**Am Anfang der Stunde**	**Al principio de la clase**
Sit down	Asseyez-vous!/ Assieds-toi!	Setzt euch!/ Setz dich!	Sentaos!/ Siéntate!
Be quiet	Taisez-vous!/ Tais-toi!	Seid still!/ Sei still!	Silencio!
Take your exercise books/books/things	Prenez vos cahiers/ vos livres/vos affaires!	Nehmt eure Hefte/ Bücher/Sachen ...	Abrid vuestros cuadernos/libros
Quiet, please	Silence, s'il vous plaît!	Ruhe, bitte!	¡Silencio por favor! ¿Quién quiere venir

Who wants to come to the board?	Qui veut venir au tableau?	Wer möchte zur Tafel kommen?	a la pizarra?
Who will come to the board?	Qui vient au tableau?	Wer kommt zur Tafel?	
Who wants to write the date?	Qui veut écrire la date?	Wer möchte das Datum schreiben?	¿Quién quiere escribir la fecha ?
Who will write the date?	Qui écrit la date?	Wer schreibt uns das Datum heute?	
Come here	Viens ici!	Komm her!	Ven!
Get up	Levez-vous!/ Lève-toi!	Steht auf!/ Steh auf!	¡Levantaos!/ ¡Levántate!
During the lesson	**Pendant le cours**	**Im Laufe des Unterrichts**	**Durante la clase**
Close the door, please	Ferme la porte, s'il te plaît!	Mach bitte die Tür zu!	Cierra la puerta por favor!
Open the window, please	Ouvre la fenêtre, s'il te plaît!	Mach das Fenster auf, bitte!	Abre la ventana por favor
Open your book at page X	Ouvrez vos livres page X	Macht eure Bücher auf! Seite X	Abrid vuestros libros a la página X por favor
Your go	C'est à toi!	Du bist dran!	Te toca a ti
Hurry up	Dépêchez-vous!/ Dépêche-toi!	Macht schnell! Beeilt euch!/Aber schnell! Beeil dich!	¡Date prisa!/¡Daos prisa!
Who wants to answer?	Qui veut répondre?	Wer möchte beantworten?	¿Quién quiere dar la respuesta?
Listen	Ecoutez bien!	Hört gut zu!	¡Escuchad bíen!
Repeat together	Répétez tous ensemble!	Wiederholt! Alle zusammen!	¡Repetid todos juntos!
Off you go	Allez-y!	Los!	¡Idos!
Draw	Dessinez!	Zeichnet!	¡Dibujad!
Look at the pictures	Regardez bien les images	Seht euch die Bilder an!	¡Mirad los dibujos! ¡Escuchad los

Listen to the dialogues and fill in the gaps	Ecoutez bien les dialogues et complétez	Hört gut zu und füllt die Lücken aus!	diálogos y rellenad los espacios!
Colour in	Coloriez!	Malt die Bilder aus!	¡Coloread!
Yes, OK	Oui, d'accord	Ja, richtig	Sí, de acuerdo
Very good	Très bien!	Sehr gut!	Muy bien
That's right	C'est bien!	Das ist gut	Exacto
Perfect	Parfait!	Ausgezeichnet!	Perfecto
Well done	C'est bon!		¡Bien hecho!
		Das ist gut so	
Yes, that's it. It's correct	Oui, c'est ça. C'est juste	Ja, gut. Richtig	Eso sí que es correcto
Of course	Bien sûr!		¡Claro!
		Ja, sicher	
Well done	Bravo!	Bravo!	
Excellent	Excellent!	Prima!	¡Excelente!
Pay attention	Faites attention	Jetzt passt auf!	¡Atención por favor!
No, pay attention	Non, attention!	Nein, passt auf!	¡No, atención por favor!
That's wrong	Ça ne va pas	Nein, das geht doch nicht	No es correcto
Please give me …	Donne-moi …, s'il te plaît	Gib mir, bitte …!	Dáme/Dadme por favor …
Could you give/lend me …?	Tu peux me donner/ prêter …?	Kannst du mir ein/e/ en …geben/ borgen?	Dáme/Dadme … préstame/préstadme
	Tu me donnes me prêtes …?	Gibst du mir/borgst du mir ein/e/en …?	
We're going to play/ sing …	On va jouer/chanter … ensemble	Wir spielen/singen … zusammen	Vamos a jugar/ cantar …
Did you understand?	Vous avez bien compris?/Compris?	Habt ihr alle verstanden?/ Verstanden?	¿Entendisteis?

Who wants to ask a question?	Qui veut poser une question?	Wer möchte eine Frage stellen?	¿Quién quiere hacer una pregunta?
	Qui pose une question?	Wer stellt eine Frage?	
Who will reply?	Qui veut répondre?	Wer möchte antworten?	¿Quién quiere contestar?
	Qui répond?	Wer weiß/gibt die Antwort?	De nuevo
Again	Encore une fois	Noch einmal!	Trabajad en pares/ en grupos de dos/ tres/ cuatro
Work in twos/ threes/ fours …	Travaillez par deux/ trois/quatre	Arbeitet zu zweit/ zu dritt/zu viert …	¡Uno por vez!
One at a time, please	Un à la fois, s'il vous plaît	Nur einer, bitte!/ Nicht alle auf einmal!	

At the end of the lesson	**A la fin du cours**	**Am Ende der Stunde**	**Al fin de la clase**
The lesson's over	C'est fini	So, jetzt machen wir Schluss	Parad ahora mismo
You've worked well	Vous avez bien travaillé	Ihr habt sehr gut gearbeitet	Has/habeis trabajado muy bien hoy
Clear up your things, please	Rangez vos affaires, s'il vous plaît	Räumt eure Sachen auf!	Recoged vuestras cosas por favor
Clear up the classroom, please	Rangez la classe, s'il vous plaît	Aufräumen, bitte!	Recógelo todo por favor
Goodbye	Au revoir!	Auf Wiedersehen!	¡Hasta pronto!
	Salut!	Tschüs!	
See you tomorrow	A demain!	Bis morgen!	¡Hasta mañana!
Until next time	A la prochaine fois!	Bis zum nächsten Mal!	¡Hasta el proxima día!
See you next Thursday	A jeudi!	Bis Donnerstag!	¡Hasta el jueves!
Have a good weekend!	Bon weekend!	Schönes Wochenende!	¡Buen fin de semana!

References

Biriotti, L. (1999) Young Pathfinder 8: *Grammar is fun!* CILT.

Biriotti, L. (2001) ResourceFile 3: *Getting the basics right: Nouns, gender and adjectives.* CILT.

Burningham, J. (1970) *Mr Gumpy's outing.* Jonathan Cape.

Büttner, S. and Alberti, J. (1996) *Tamburin 1* and *2.* Max Hueber Verlag/European Schoolbooks.

Carle, E. (1970) *The very hungry caterpillar.* Hamish Hamilton.

Challier, H. and Gavelli, S. (1995) *Gaston 1* and *2.* ELI/European Schoolbooks.

Challier, H. and Gavelli, S. (1999) *Avant Gaston: cours préparatoire.* ELI/European Schoolbooks.

Cheater, C. and Farren, A. (2001) Young Pathfinder 9:*The literacy link.* CILT.

CILT (2001) *European Language Portfolio.* CILT.

CILT (2001) *Making it happen (Early Language Learning video 1).* CILT.

CILT (2002) *Making it work (Early Language Learning video 2).* CILT.

CILT (2003) *Making it better (Early Language Learning video 3).* CILT.

Council of Europe (1996) *Common European Framework for Language Learning.* Council of Europe.

Datta, M., Pomphrey, C. (2004) Young Pathfinder 10: *A world of languages: Developing children's love of language.* CILT.

de Silva, J. and Satchwell, P. (1995) Young Pathfinder 1: *Catching them young.* CILT.

DfES (2002) *National Language Strategy. Languages for all: Languages for life – a strategy for England.* DfES.

Dobson, P. and Cantley, R. (1998) *Story telling through pictures.* MLG Publishing.

Elston, J. (2000) ResourceFile 2: *Up, up and away! Using classroom target language to help learners say what they want to say.* CILT.

Farren, A. and Smith, R. (2003) *Bringing it home.* CILT.

Gerngross, G., Krenn, W. and Puchta, H. (2003) *Ja klar!* ELI/European Schoolbooks.

Gobbi, R. and Bouard, C. (2000, 2001, 2001) *Hélico et ses copains 1, 2, 3.* ELI/European Schoolbooks.

Goethe-Institut (1996) *Nürnberg recommendations on early language learning.* Goethe-Institut.

Hicks, D. (2002) *Les chansons et les raps de Monsieur X.* David Hicks, Impington Village College.

Hawkins, E. (1987) Foreign languages in the curriculum. Cambridge University Press.

Husar, B. (1999) *1, 2, 3 techno.* European Schoolbooks.

Husar, B. (1996) *1, 2, 3 soleil!*. European Schoolbooks.

Johnstone, R. (1994a) *Modern Languages in the primary school – competences*. SOED.

Johnstone, R. (1994b) *Teaching Modern Languages at primary school*. SCRE.

La Jolie Ronde (1996) *Entre dans la ronde*. LJR Educational.

Martin, C. (1995) Young Pathfinder 2: *Games and fun activities*. CILT.

Martin, C. (2002) ResourceFile 6: *Rhythm and rhyme: Developing language in French and German*. CILT.

Martin, C. and Cheater C. (1998) Young Pathfinder 6: *Let's join in! Rhymes, poems, songs*. CILT.

Martin, C. and Farren, A. (2004) Young Pathfinder 12: *Working together: Native speakers in the primary school*. CILT.

May, S., and Richardson, P. (1998) *Fieldwork in action 6: Crossing the channel*. Geographical Association.

McColl, H., Thomas, S. (1997) *Ici on parle français: French for beginners*. MLG Publishing.

McColl, H., Thomas, S. and Satchwell, P. (1999) *Wir sprechen Deutsch: German for beginners*. MLG Publishing.

McColl, H., Thomas, S., and López-Océn, T. (2000) *Se habla español: Spanish for beginners*. MLG Publishing.

Mireylees, J. and Hallam, C. (1998) *Chante Noël!* Merryman Primary Resources.

Mireylees, J., Pryce, J. and Shaw, M. (1999) *Ouvre la porte!* Merryman Primary Resources.

Primary Languages Network (1997) 'The introduction of foreign languages into the primary school curriculum'. A consultation paper sent to DfEE.

QCA. *Scheme of work for languages at KS2* (2000). QCA.

Rowe, I. and Kilberry, I. (1995) *3, 2, 1 ... los!* KETV.

Rowe, I. and Kilberry, I. (1999, 2002) *Early Start Spanish:* Part 1: *Tú y yo*; Part 2: *Mi ciudad y mi colegio*. Early Start Languages.

Rowe, I. and Kilberry, I. (2001) *Early Start French*. Early Start Languages.

Rumley, G., Rowe, I. and Kilberry, I. (1992, 1993, 1993) *Pilote 1, 2* and *3*. KETV.

Satchwell, P. (1997) Young Pathfinder 4: *Keep talking! Teaching in the target language*. CILT.

Sharpe, K. (2001) *Modern Foreign Languages in the primary school: The what, why and how of early MFL teaching*. Kogan Page.

Schimek, F. (1997) Senior Schools' Inspector, Vienna.

Skarbek, C. (1998) Young Pathfinder 5: *First steps to reading and writing*. CILT.

Tierney, D. and Dobson, M. (1995) Young Pathfinder 3: *Are you sitting comfortably? Telling stories to young learners*. CILT.

Tierney, D. and Hope, M. (1998) Young Pathfinder 7: *Making the link*. CILT.

Williams, R. and Leclerq-Hallam, C. (2002) *La ronde des petits: French for 3–5 year-olds*. La Jolie Ronde.